BMW
6 Series

Enthusiast's Companion

by Jeremy Walton

RB

ROBERT BENTLEY
PUBLISHERS

BMW 6 Series

Dixi was the brand name before BMW took over 1928. See Chapter 1.

This 328 could reach speeds of nearly 140 mph. See Chapter 2.

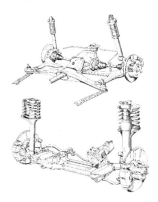

The 5 Series origins of the 6 Series. See Chapter 3

633CSi in Federal 3.2-liter form. See Chapter 5.

The Federal version of the
635 motor. See Chapter 6.

The 24-valve M5 engine.
See Chapter 8.

Dieter Quester in the 1986
635 car. See Chapter 9.

The author's 635, also
known as Helga. See
Chapter 10.

 **ROBERT BENTLEY, INC.** | AUTOMOTIVE PUBLISHERS

Information that makes
the difference.®

1734 Massachusetts Avenue
Cambridge, MA 02138 USA
800-423-4595 / 617-547-4170
http://www.rb.com
e-mail: sales@rb.com

Copies of this book may be purchased from selected booksellers, or directly from the publisher by mail. The publisher encourages comments from the reader of this book. Please write to Robert Bentley, Inc., Publishers at the address listed on the top of this page.

Library of Congress Cataloging-in-Publication Data

Walton, Jeremy, 1946-
BMW 6 Series: enthusiast's companion / Jeremy Walton.
      p.   cm.
Includes index.
ISBN: 0-8376-0149-5
1. BMW automobiles.   I. Title.
TL215.B25W348523   1999
388.3'422--dc21   99-29313
                                                            CIP

Bentley Stock No. GBM6
02 01 00 99 10 9 8 7 6 5 4 3 2 1

BMW 6 Series Enthusiast's Companion, by Jeremy Walton

This book is dedicated to
Mrs. Vera Grace Walton
(1909–1998)

Foreword

When the 6 Series was created in the seventies, motor cars were less complex than today. Today this beautiful coupe still turns heads and attracts admiration for it's handsome lines.

Inspect any 6 Series closely and you will see the cockpit was very advanced: easy to use with many electronic features-such as the Service Interval Indicator and on-board computer/check systems-that have improved smaller BWM's today. Under the hood were a variety of the famous BMW inline six cylinders, including one version with the 24-valve layout that we expect of our contemporary cars.

So the 6 Series was a genuine pathfinder in many of the features that we accept as normal today, but the 6 Series was not just a beautiful body. The proven performance of the rugged running gear beneath that 2-door silhouette was so strong that it could take all the cruel loads that motorsport inflicts, and finish a winner.

Twice the 635CSi won European Championships against vastly more powerful opposition, and it added to BMW's unmatched record amongst touring cars in the most demanding 24 hour events of Germany's Nürburgring and Spa in Belgium.

The 6 Series truly was a classic BMW, combining competition pedigree with a thoroughbred elegance that still enthuses owners all over the world. The "Six" may not be on our production lines at this time, but it is not forgotten...

Gerhard Berger
BMW Competition Director
and retired Grand Prix/6 Series racing driver

Munich, Germany, Autumn 1998

Introduction

Before we begin, here is some introductory background on this publication, which covers all 6 Series coupe BMWs manufactured between 1976–89. Finally there are some acknowledgments to complete.

The standpoint is that of an interested nineties owner(1986 635CSi), one who had written an eight chapter book on the handsome Bimmer. This monochrome title, (*High Performance Series: BMW 6 Series*) was published in 1984 Britain.

That eighties book could not cover post-1984 production 6 Series developments, and had long been out of print. No current trading trace could be found of its original publisher. Both Robert Bentley Publishers, who published my first American-based BMW book: *Unbeatable BMW*, and myself were constantly frustrated when potential customers asked "Why no 6 Series title? We need this book NOW."

A lot of background work in 1996–98 has made this volume possible. This 6 Series title was created by the original author totally rewriting from the original text, adding what had been learned in the ensuing 17 years and locating fresh picture sources.

I had the advantage of hindsight, knowing that the following 8 Series was not accepted by BMW enthusiasts as a replacement for the "Sixer". Hottest rumor at press time was that a totally new 6 Series line would replace the slower selling 8 Series, shortly after the millennium.

JW.

QUICK FACTS

Period
1896–1983

Products
Saucepans to 6 Series

Low points
Two World Wars and 1959–60 insolvency

High points
"No pain, no gain" approach led
to the 6 Series

1

BMW: Masters of Multiple Re-invention

The twisting tale of how BMW became what it is today, ranging over land, sea and air

Before the birth of the sleek and shining 6 Series coupe for the seventies and eighties, the Bayerische Motoren Werke (source of those now prestigious initials) suffered a convoluted and often painful birth of its own, mastering the art of reinventing itself to meet each new challenge. For BMW evolved from a dozen different origins, even prior to the first use of those initials to designate a new force in aircraft engine manufacture starting on March 7, 1916.

The researcher is faced with myriad deals, financial crises, and two World Wars that directly affected BMW's fortunes. You have to admire the company's survival, never mind its present awesome prosperity as the manufacturer of more than half a million vehicles a year, of which more than one hundred thousand annually reach the US, and more than half that number are delivered to the UK. Equally impressive are profits of the kind that financed the four-cylinder world headquarters opposite Munich's Olympiapark.

Can this BMW of the nineties, now with established production facilities in the US and the owners of the Rover Group in the UK, really be the same company that had to make saucepans from aluminum scraps? Since BMW faced the full fury of allied airborne weaponry in the fourties, the company has reinvented itself over seven major production centers to meet the strong demand for their motorcar and motorcycle products.

This epitome of West German postwar revival was the same BMW which faced corporate life as a mere Mercedes division in 1959. Back then, BMW reeled onto the ringside ropes of motor manufacturing, deploying a model mix that plunged from low-volume, hand-crafted V8s to Isetta-

Honored at Spartan-
burg, South Carolina,
BMW North America's
preserved Federal 6
Series sits among such
diverse company land-
marks as the 1.5-liter
motor, a dissected speci-
men of the breed that
won the world's first turbocharged Formula 1
title. Contrast its 1200
horsepower capabilities
with those of the econ-
omy Isetta alongside, or
the 2002 with typically
sporty modifications and
a classic 328 open two-
seater.

In late October 1997,
Spartanburg built the
100,000th Z3. By con-
trast, during the entire
1976–89 span of the 6
Series, just 86,216
examples of BMW's
premiere coupe were
constructed.

Picture: Author
June 1997

BMW bubble cars. It was also true that these providers of the supremely
logical 3, 5, 6, and 7 Series were once affiliated with Eastern Germany's
Wartburg manufacturing site at Eisenach. It might further surprise you to
discover that BMW started car manufacture with a license to make spin-
dly British Austin Sevens?

All these factual statements reflect BMW's tortuous history. Whether
manufacturing aircraft engines for wartime use or producing the kind of
cars and motorcycles that attract its legendary, fierce customer loyalty,
BMW's title is absolutely apt. Bavarian Motor Works makes superb
engines that really have made a mark on land, sea, and air history.

If we look back through the company records, the constant competitive
element is always present, whether in outright wartime conditions or in
the eighties 6 Series era as the 600–1,200 bhp turbo powerhouse behind
1983 Brabham-BMW World Champion Nelson Piquet. They really are
supreme competitors down in Bavaria....

Birth of the 6 Series

The subject of this book, the two-door 6 Series coupe, illustrates BMW
tradition well. Originally, it was conceived as an upmarket move from the
popular Karmann-bodied sporting coupes of 1968–75. This series of two-
door coupes had set the racing world on its ear with the use of a "Batmobile" wing set for CSL competition models-race cars that eventually bore
mighty Munich 24-valve motors that delivered 470 horsepower.

BMW decided that a touch more civilization was needed in the 6 Series successor and, using the 5 Series sedan as a literal base, it created a line of luxury coupes of increased refinement and creature comfort. Initially culminating in a 3.3-liter, fuel-injection 633CSi , the 6 Series range showed a flexibility to adopt increased power that is the hallmark of a well-balanced design.

Within a couple of years, BMW was forced to offer customers the performance expected of their heritage, qualities the original 6 Series failed to deliver. BMW returned to its sporting heritage with the 635CSi, a 135-mph-plus derivative that used the cylinder block of the previously "racing-only" 3.5-liter size created by BMW Motorsport engine supremo Paul Rosche's versatile staff. It was not long before the 635 was notching up European sedan championship titles with the same abandon as the earlier coupes, but the American market was still shortchanged on power output in Federal-emissions guise.

Finally, the European 6 Series returned even more powerfully to remind us of earlier BMW racing success. The M-for-Motorsport 635CSi housed a 286 bhp version of the 24-valve engine first seen in the M1, rated 256 horsepower in the US and usually dubbed "M6" although that badge was never an official one in Europe.

The M635 gave BMW a 150-mph "M6" coupe to prowl Porsche-invested autobahns with pride. As we shall see, that remarkable quad-valve-per-cylinder six-cylinder went through many development stages between M635 duty and its original role as provider of growling supercar performance in the mid-engined M1 of 1978-81. Throughout our story, the respect BMW earned as suppliers of supremely appealing power plants in conscientiously crafted automobiles was apparent.

There have been mistakes, some of them in far more public competition arenas than many rivals were prepared to contest. Still, when you look over the solid worth of the 6 Series, it is obvious that BMW created a superb coupe—one worthy of its fascinating heritage. I have learned this firsthand, as this book was written alongside the 1997–98 restoration of my own 1986 635CSi.

Roots

Tracing the origins of BMW in car manufacture means traveling to the East of Germany and the historic castle town of Eisenach. Here in Thuringia's forested and hilly terrain, armament specialist and multi-talented inventor Dr. Heinriech Ehrhardt formed Fahrzeugfabrik Eisenach on December 3, 1896. Dr. Ehrhardt had already played a prominent role in

The Dixi name as it
appeared at the 1904
Frankfurt Motor Show.

the emergence of Rhinemetall Konzern, second in scale only to Krupp in armament manufacturing within Germany.

In view of their connections, it was not surprising that the first Eisenach vehicles were military designs, such as munitions carriers, ambulance, and gun carriages; but these ventures were not an overwhelming financial success. Thus, in 1898, Ehrhardt foresaw modern motor industry practice and agreed with Decauville in France to make a small voiturette class of car.

By the turn of the century, Eisenach was using the emblem, and the name, of the Wartburg Castle that watches over the town of Eisenach. Even in 1899, BMW's Wartburg forebears were racing up to the then-enormous speed of 37 mph (it sounds much faster when you say 60 km/h!). Wartburgs were also winning attention at the Berlin motor shows of the period, and even got around to exporting a machine known as the Cosmobile to the US.

From 1889 to 1903, it is estimated that about 250 Wartburg cars were delivered from Eisenach, many under the Decauville agreement, but Wartburgs also came in fierce racing guises. In 1902, they had four-cylinder motors delivering some 22 bhp from 3.1 liters, and the sophistication of a five-speed gearbox to enable them to reach slightly beyond Britain's 70-mph limit of 82 years later.

Ehrhardt resigned the chair of Eisenach in 1903 to form his own company away from Rhinemetall, who also got rid of the embryo Wartburg outfit. Dixi was the brand name used by the Eisenach Motorworks in the early 1900's, and it continued until BMW took over financial control in 1928. The Dixi name was confirmed at the 1904 Frankfurt Motor Show (today the biggest motor show in Europe), with a touring car displayed for this important hardy annual.

Dixi evolved from 1904 to 1927, manufacturing giant 7.3-liter racing and touring cars en route, along with trucks that naturally found increased demand through World War I. After hostilities concluded, Eisenach's Dixi marque was in trouble, along with much of the rest of German industry. The takeover trail that leads to BMW today began here.

First Gothaer Wagonfabrik took on the Eisenach manufacturers, but they were in no fit state to resist the advances of a well-known contemporary financier, Jacob Schapiro. Look through the histories of NSU and Mercedes/Daimler-Benz, and you will find he was involved with them, as well as other now-defunct marques such as Cyklon and Hansa. Altogether, 15,822 vehicles were reckoned to have been made at Eisenach before BMW stepped in on October 1, 1928. Now, let us look back to see where the men of Munich generated enough revenue in the inflation-stricken Germany of the 1920s to afford a debt-ridden Dixi empire....

By 1912, Dixi was an established marque, and their cars were well-respected by the German middle classes. That season, they made 259 splendid motor carriages, aided by such grand press advertisements as this example.

Drawing re-published 1978 via Werner Oswald

Again, military contracts feature in such history, together with two Austrians and a German from the Swabian district that encompasses the home of Mercedes and Porsche in Stuttgart. Austrian engineering graduate Franz Joseph Popp was sent to study aircraft engineering manufacturing techniques at Daimler and Benz in 1914, with a view to making such motors at the works of his employers, AEG-Union in Vienna. The plan did not reach fruition, but Popp learned enough to want to be further involved. Ironically the change came in the form of a marine authority engine contract for aircraft engines awarded to Rapp Motor Works in Munich, which Popp was asked to oversee.

The young Popp (he was under twenty at the outbreak of World War I) did not like what he saw in terms of the incompetence displayed by Rap's production methods. Popp enlisted the help of a man who really can take the credit for much of BMW's early power-plant engineering reputation: Dr. Max Friz. Popp and Friz were bankrolled by Camillo Castiglioni and were all set for a career in the provision of wartime aeronautical engines. Friz was a former Daimler designer who had brought with him the concept of a high-performance aircraft engine, after a pay dispute with his former employers at Daimler.

For the purist, it should be noted that there were two 1916 dates that the featured formation of companies entitled to use BMW initials: July 20, 1916 saw the creation of Bayerische Motorwerke GmbH from the unified Gustav Rau and Rapp Motorenwerke. Yet today's company name, proudly displayed over the portals of the four-cylinder building, Bayerischen

BMW's roots in mass
manufacture grew
from these drawings!
The primitive appear-
ance of the original
right-hand-drive Austin
7-derived Dixi and its
crude frame chassis
disguised a leading-
edge design among
1920s European econ-
omy cars. This is the
15-horsepower BMW
DA2 development, its
steering established on
the left side. Top speed
was just over 45 mph,
but the reward was
more than 40 miles to
a gallon of gas.

Drawing: BMW Archiv
Released 1979

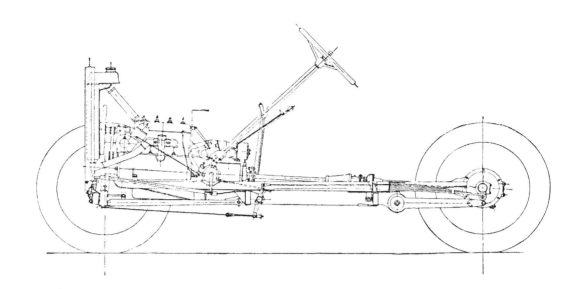

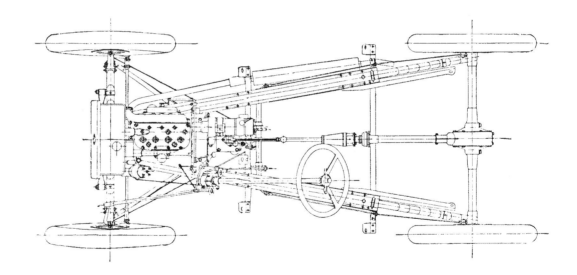

Motoren Werke AG, came when Castiglioni purchased the Lerchenauer Strasse site next to the postwar defunct Bavarian Airplane Works. They entered the name that is used today in the Munich city register on that March 7, 1916 date we gave earlier. Confused? There's more to come....

The end of the war saw BMW with less than 100 of the planned 2,000 Friz-designed BMW 111a aircraft engines delivered, and a ban on further German manufacture of such power-plants. It got by with various static motors and the fabrication of railway braking systems, but the BMW of today became recognizable when the Friz flat-twin motorcycle motor joined the R32 double-tube frame bike, along with shaft drive. These principles live on in the nineties, although it is worth noting that BMW motorcycles are not manufactured in Munich, but in Berlin. This was also true for the new four-cylinder K-series, as well as the flat-twin descendants of the Friz era, which commenced manufacture in 1923.

BMW was back in the aircraft business for engine manufacture by 1924, but chief engineer and co-founder Franz Popp wanted a further diversification into the small car business. BMW looked at a number of existing options, including a front-drive, boxer, opposed-cylinder machine; principles shared with BMW motorcycle philosophy were an obvious attraction.

When BMW opted out of this Schwabischen Hutten Werke (SHW) prototype series, there was an opportunity to acquire Dixi at Eisenach. Like most others in Germany in the 1920s, BMW was pretty near broke in the conventional banking sense. Financial magician Camillo Castiglioni performed in his customarily persuasive manner, and the share capital was upped some 60 percent to allow BMW financial control at Eisenach during November 1928, although the deal was actually recognized when Dixi at Eisenach became a BMW subsidiary from October 1 of that year.

With the 1,200 Dixi employees came a ready-made production car that BMW decided to keep on, and which eventually became the first BMW four-wheeler. The machine was known as the Dixi 3/15, but it was actually a modified Austin Seven that the wheeling-and-dealing Schapiro had acquired for Dixi when they could no longer afford to develop its own machinery.

The first 100 Austin Sevens came direct from the UK and were on sale by April 1927, complete with right-hand drive (RHD)! When production commenced in Germany, however, left-hand drive (LHD) was installed, along with such sophisticated developments as battery ignition. Such cars were made late in 1927 and were sold starting in January 1928.

When BMW took over, it left the Dixi badge and the car alone until July 1929, when the BMW badge and a series of changes showed that

Just 12,052 of these BMW 3/15 DA2 running chassis (built under a variety of bodies) were made from July 1929 to 1930, when it was updated. Altogether, BMW with Dixi made 25,256 similar four cylinders in the 1927–32 period, produced with increasing independence from the earlier British design.

Picture: BMW Archiv
Released 1979

Clothing the 3/15 more glamorously involved a number of specialist coachbuilders. This is the Ihle sports two-seater of 1930, and it was this Karlsruhe company that inaugurated BMW's most famous body design trademark: the *Nierenformen* (kidney shaped) front grille. The first BMW to wear this divided grille was the 303 of summer 1933, which also premiered BMW's first series production in-line six-cylinder engine.

Picture: Author
June 1997

the new masters were restless to exploit their own engineering ideas for light cars.

Gradually modifying the Seven concept further and further-including a batch of derivatives for army use and a rather unpleasant swing front axle—BMW tramped inexorably toward a true BMW car. By 1932, it had delivered over 25,000 Seven cousins, but in March, it terminated the licensing agreement to go its own way.

That spring, BMW brought its own 3/20 design to the market, which still had a small (782 cc) four-cylinder now producing 20 bhp at 3,500 rpm. It had overhead valves (OHV) rather than the Seven's side-valve setup, which had provided 15 horsepower at 3,000 rpm on the same cheap-fuel 5.6:1 compression ratio. Ah, those were the low-stress days....

The first BMW had a three-speed gearbox and would reach around 50 mph, with BMW sources recalling 37 mpg as typical of its everyday fuel consumption. It weighed a lot more than the earlier Seven-derived cars, its body built by Daimler-Benz at Sindelfingen. In those pre-World War II days, Stuttgart, Munich, and Eisenach management were on exceptionally friendly terms. After all, there was

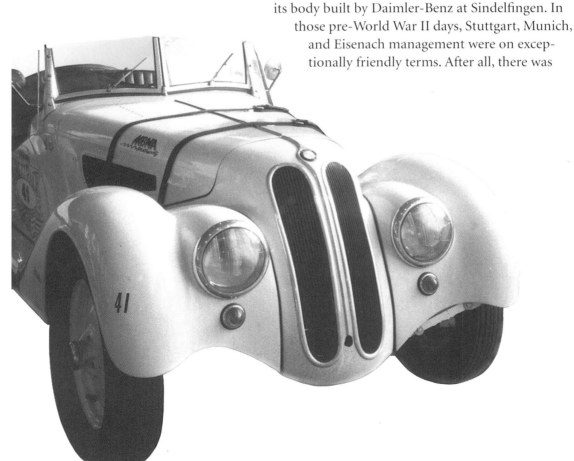

The favorite classic BMW of all time appears to be the 328 open sports roadster of 1936–39. Just 464 were built, and there was no better balanced 2-liter of the prewar period. An astounding motorsports winner from its June 1936 debut at the Nürburgring onward, the 328 lines inspired many more commercially successful British sports cars of the 1950s. BMW's six-cylinder engine powered many other marques and was developed from a street 80 bhp to 136 racing horsepower.

Picture: Author
June 1997

plenty of military aviation work for everyone as the emphasis on military manufacturing returned in Germany.

BMW had returned to its first love of performance aircraft engines, as can be seen by analyzing its 1933 staff employment records: over half were working on aircraft engines. As World War II approached, BMW diversi-fied its military activities well beyond engine manufacture, but the car business was far from neglected in the 1930s.

BMW's increasing prosperity allowed further funds for car develop-ment. The six-cylinder, in-line engine design that would lead to the now-collectable 328 classic sports car traced its roots to the 1933 BMW 303. This was a modest sedan, but it ran smoothly and sweetly to its 62-mph (100-kmh) maximum. This BMW six-cylinder, the smallest I can recall, offered 30 bhp delivered via the usual long stroke (56 x 80 mm gave 1,173 cc).

The six-cylinders continued in the 1934-37 BMW 315, with 1,490 cc and 34 horsepower. The 315 had a sporting 315/1 brother, with the same cubic capacity, which featured triple sidedraft Solex carburetors and a 6.8:1 compression ratio, a sharp increase over the former Austin ratio of 5.6:1. This sport version brought 40 bhp at 4,300 rpm and a capacity for tackling newly constructed autobahns at speeds of 75 mph—pretty impressive for 60 years ago, and faster than most speed limits enforced in the US and UK today. Envy would be the relevant emotion to feel for the 230 or so lucky 315/1 owners and their rakish two-seaters, for they were the sporting forerunners of the many desirable performance products that BMW subsequently created.

There were plenty of other six-cylinder models made by BMW in com-paratively small numbers at Eisenach in the 1930s. These included the 319/1, which gave 55 bhp from the 1,911-cc engine it shared with the less-exotically carbureted 319 and 329. But the most interest was generated then-and today-by the perfectly balanced package of sporting qualities presented in the BMW 328.

"Announced" by Ernst Henne, pounding around the Nürburgring to class victory in the Eifelrennen races of June 1936, the 328 was sold start-ing in February 1937 with a choice of four-speed gearboxes, including one from BMW 6 Series supplier ZF. In production, the 328 BMWsix-cylinder had a capacity of 1,971 cc from a bore and stroke of 66 x 96 mm. Com-plete with a unique pushrod valve-gear operation that allowed the quali-ties of overhead-camshaft engineering to be previewed on the in-line six-cylinder, the 328 set new standards of efficiently enjoyable motoring. For the period, compression was set high at 7.6:1. Feeding from three Solex 30-mm downdraft carburetors, it punched out 80 bhp at 5,000 rpm.

The Road to 6 Series

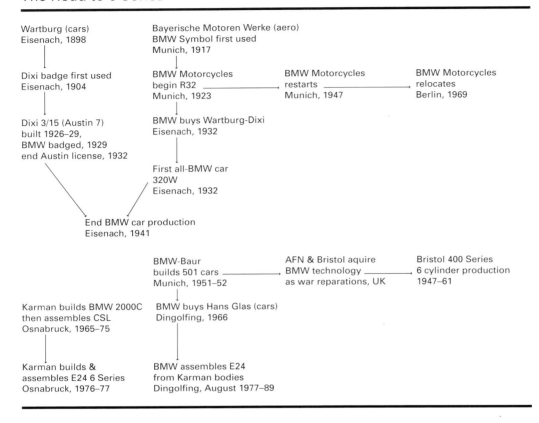

Wartburg (cars)
Eisenach, 1898

Bayerische Motoren Werke (aero)
BMW Symbol first used
Munich, 1917

Dixi badge first used
Eisenach, 1904

BMW Motorcycles
begin R32
Munich, 1923

BMW Motorcycles
restarts
Munich, 1947

BMW Motorcycles
relocates
Berlin, 1969

Dixi 3/15 (Austin 7)
built 1926–29,
BMW badged, 1929
end Austin license, 1932

BMW buys Wartburg-Dixi
Eisenach, 1932

First all-BMW car
320W
Eisenach, 1932

End BMW car production
Eisenach, 1941

BMW-Baur
builds 501 cars
Munich, 1951–52

AFN & Bristol aquire
BMW technology
as war reparations, UK

Bristol 400 Series
6 cylinder production
1947–61

Karman builds BMW 2000C
then assembles CSL
Osnabruck, 1965–75

BMW buys Hans Glas (cars)
Dingolfing, 1966

Karman builds &
assembles E24 6 Series
Osnabruck, 1976–77

BMW assembles E24
from Karman bodies
Dingolfing, August 1977–89

That power output was enough to realize 93 mph with 20 mpg fuel consumption. However, most of the 462 BMW 328s manufactured had modifications of some sort applied-if not during the 1930s, then almost certainly during subsequent years, when a lot of 328 technology reemerged in various guises as European and (rarer) American enthusiasts endeavored to enjoy motorsports once more.

For BMW, getting back on its feet after World War II would probably be the hardest task ever faced by this resourceful concern. Certainly, among German-based automobile factories, BMW had the toughest task in resuming motor-car manufacture. The main Munich works at Milbertshofen had been a major Allied-forces target for saturation-bombing techniques. The USAAF and the RAF maintained night-and-day bombing missions, razing most of the facility to the ground. Eisenach subsequently fell under the rule of the East Germany-based Soviet Army. This looked to be the worst possible news, but in 1945, Eisenach began to produce sedans based on prewar designs, beating BMW at Munich to the production punch by almost ten years. The first postwar Eisenach products were based on the rugged 1,971-cc six-cylinder, branded Autovelo BMW 321.

It took BMW, regrouped in Munich and Brandenburg (Berlin) after the loss of Eisenach, until 1947 to resume motorcycle manufacture in the form of the R24. Prior to this, BMW was forced to survive by making cooking utensils, repairing vehicles, and generally salvaging any metal fabrication work that could be disinterred from the ruins. Even such simple tasks were a major achievement because US-occupied Munich had originally received instructions that BMW was to be broken beyond recognition and subject to complete confiscation of all assets.

Thus, in the immediate postwar years, BMW could only sit on the sidelines while concerns such as the Bristol Aircraft Company in Britain were awarded "the spoils of war" in the form of the remaining six-cylinder power-plants and drawings. Bristol subsequently developed the 2-liter engine to much higher production power outputs (105 bhp from their hand-built 405) and stretched the unit to 2.2 liters for the Bristol 406, which did not cease production until 1961. BMW engine design was thus to stay on the production and competition motoring scene over four totally different decades! Incidentally, the link between Bristol, aviation interests, and BMW was completed via the UK's prewar official BMW importer, AFN. H. J. Aldington was a director of Bristol and had been responsible for AFN's introduction of BMW to the British market in the 1930s. Even then, BMW went to the trouble of re-engineering RHD for the limited number of vehicles sent to the UK. AFN subsequently became the Porsche importer for Great Britain, disillusioned by BMW's uneven product output in the 1950s.

BMW in Munich also had to exhume the 1,971-cc, 6-cylinder engine for its first postwar model, the 501 sedan. This rotund machine had a unique beveled-gear steering system and a gearbox mounted virtually under the front seats, connected forward by a stubby propshaft. It was shown at the Frankfurt Salon of 1951, despite the fact that BMW had no machine tools to stamp its body pressings! BMW managed to make the first 501s on a stout tubular chassis during 1952, using the facilities of Baur at Stuttgart. The latter was to contribute much to the mid-engined M1 construction during 1978-81 as well. BMW's own pressed-steel facilities were not onstream until 1955.

These 65-horsepower 501 sedans could waddle up to 84 mph, despite their 2,948-lb (1,340-kg) girth. Understandably, it took a 501 about 27 seconds to reach 62 mph (100 kmh) from rest, an acceleration figure that could not even match prewar levels. Germany's first postwar production

V8, also unique in its aluminum-alloy construction, solved the 501's pace problems from 1954 onward. The BMW V8 offered an initial 90 bhp, but that figure rose to 160 bhp in the 1962-65 ancestors of the subsequent BMW 3200CS coupes.

The 90-degree V8 engine began production at a capacity of 2,580 cc, featuring virtually square bore and stroke dimensions of 74 x 75 mm. Toward the end of its production span, the V8 measured 3,168 cc (82 x 75 mm) for the rare but extremely stylish 503 and 507 sporting designs of 1956-59. Both were styled by long-time New York resident Albrecht Graf von Goertz, and were based on the 501/502 sedan running gear. They established a postwar BMW tradition for sporting cousins of production sedans that was most commercially successful in the coupes of the 1960s, 1970s, and 1980s, or the Z3 sports designs out of Spartanburg in the 1990s.

The 252 BMW 507s constructed in the 1950s were capable of stomping up to 137 mph and could cover 0-62 mph in 11.5 seconds. However the low production runs of these and other large BMWs of the immediate postwar period were obviously not going to extract Munich from increasing financial distress.

Motorcycles simply could not offset mounting losses in the car division, which offered big limousines at one end of the scale (501/2, 503/7) in stark contrast to flyweights such as the 1955-62 Isetta 250 or the 1956-62 Isetta 300 with three- and four-wheeler layouts.

There was nothing to offer to the vital middle-class market, which had emerged into a booming sector of revitalized West Germany. The 600 four-wheeler was a step in the right direction, and previewed the principles of BMW's subsequent and successful trailing-arm independent rear suspension. However, the 600 still had the feel of a modified Isetta as well as its flat-twin motorcycle engine that was also mounted in the rear of the more successful 700. The 700, in both sedan and pretty coupe editions, had to "hold the fort" until a middleweight, 1.5-liter, four-door BMW sedan could be introduced.

Losses that were apparent in 1958 had reached a crisis point by 1959. In December 1959, the Deutsche Bank proposed a radical redevelopment plan that amounted to amalgamating BMW with the Mercedes parent company, Daimler-Benz. BMW shareholders and the vociferous dealer network revolted against this strong medicine. The BMW rebels formed a coalition to fight this proposal with astonishing effectiveness under the leadership of Frankfurt lawyer Dr. Friedreich Mathern.

Aided by venture capital from neighbor MAN (the truck concern), the BMW rebels fought on until the Deutsche Bank and Mercedes withdrew,

Bayerische Motoren Werke was created to build fine fighter-plane aircraft engines and the automobiles carry on that tradition of engineering excellence. Here are two of the best: the M1 six-cylinder ancestor to the M6 motor in its original mechanical injection 277-bhp trim (the one with six shining trumpets) and the four-cylinder, which is actually the supreme Grand Prix turbo of the eighties, capable of delivering two hours of race pace at 600 bhp, or doubling that output for a brief qualifying lap!

Pictures: BMW Archiv Munich, 1978, 1980

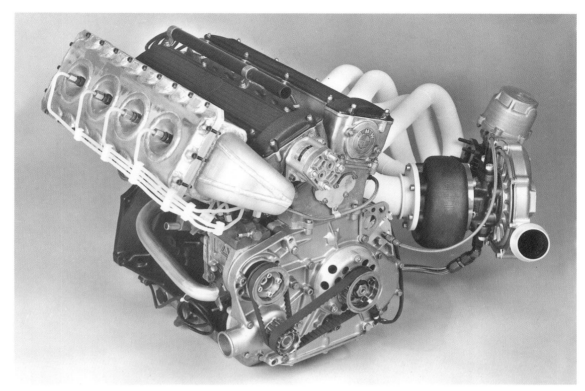

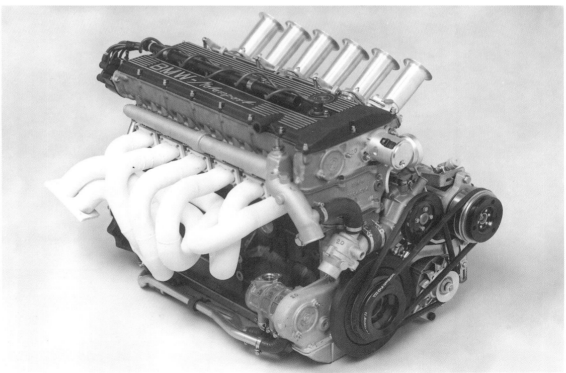

Dr. Mathern serving on the BMW board until 1966. Prime BMW investors were the Quandt brothers, Herbert and Harald, who emerged as substantial stockholders in the early 1960s. Dr. Herbert Quandt took the most personal interest in BMW and built on his stock holdings of 15% to the point where he held voting control of more than half the issued capital. Even as BMW headed for the millennium as one of the richest motor manufacturers on earth, Quandt's widow (Joanna) held significant shares of BMW and was rated one of the richest women in the world.

A general meeting in November 1960 saw BMW steered toward its present success, initially guided by Dr. Johannes Semler. He had the confidence of increased capital and an extremely warm reception for the rear-engine 700, which had debuted in 1959. The 700 sold more than 181,000 units in sedan and coupe bodies, and also founded the BMW reputation for winning with products directly related to their road cars. In the 1960s, drivers such as multiple Le Mans winner Jacky Ickx established their competition careers in 100-mph racing versions of the agile 700CS.

BMW's current marketing strength for refined front-engine, rear-drive sporting sedans stems from the September 1961 introduction of the Neue Klasse 1500. After considerable teething troubles, the February 1962 debut of the 1500 in production changed BMW fortunes for the better in less than two years. In this long-awaited mid-range contender were the key features on which the BMW manufacturing revival has been based. For example, the 1500 had an immensely strong single overhead-camshaft (SOHC) power unit with an aluminum cylinder head and an iron block. It was this cast-iron casing that withstood up to 1,200 horsepower in BMW's Brabham Grand Prix era of the 1980s. Normally raced between 600 and 850 horsepower, it was the 1.5-liter turbo powerhouse behind 1983 World Champion Nelson Piquet of Brazil.

Alex Freiherr von Falkenhausen headed the engine design team of the postwar period, a team that included subsequent father to the Grand Prix turbo engine (and many other road and race designs) Paul Rosche—nicknamed "Camshaft Paul" after his mathematical adeptness in profiling new camshaft designs. The Munich-born-and-bred Rosche was the key figure in the development of the six-cylinder motors that powered the 6 Series from two valves per cylinder to the later electronically-managed quad-valvers.

Von Falkenhausen established the basics of the 1500's layout, including the combustion-chamber shape, immense bottom-end strength, and an alloy head carrying chain drive for the overhead camshaft with a V-pattern valve gear.

The 3-series sedans from the McLaren North America/BMW NA alliance were the most relevant application of BMW turbocharged technology to the American racing world. Expat Briton David Hobbs was the most regular winner for BMW. With just four cylinders and 2.1 liters or less, BMW's major problem was to compete durably with the six-cylinder turbo Porsches of 3-liters and more.

Picture: BMW Archiv 1979

Such basics were further detailed, or suggested, by others, but it was von Falkenhausen who had the vision to combine cost-effective high technology in one tough package, ensuring that it was cheaper to make and more versatile than the DOHC designs of Alfa Romeo (then the inspiration and subsequent main competition and commercial rivals of BMW). The basic layout, including a switch to the slant-block layout that characterized all subsequent (1800 onward) four- and six-cylinder, in-line BMW motors, was effective for both units from the sixties to the eighties—some individual features (such as the 30-degree slant) are retained as we head to the millennium.

Illustrating the connection with four- and six-cylinder BMWs of the past, the 1,990-cc SOHC four-cylinder and the 2,985-cc six-cylinder were used in 3.0 coupes of the 1970s and 3.0 sedans (plus initial 6 Series models) that included the Federal US 530i. The short-stroke 80-mm bore was shared by both, and the 89-mm stroke pops up on a few occasions too.

Take a look at other BMW post-sixties four- and six-cylinder engines, and you'll find all kinds of common permutations. This is true particularly of cylinder bores, the pointer to basic strength and adaptability in design.

BMW also utilized common machine tooling for cylinder blocks, so bore sizes frequently coincided. In the period we discuss, the 528, 728, and 628 all used an 80-mm stroke. The US-import 733/633i and the previous 730/630/530, plus the subsequent European 732i and Turbo 745i, all shared an 89-mm bore.

The 1500 four-cylinder engine, uprated to 80 bhp between its show debut and production, established a BMW breed that lasted into the late eighties within the 3 Series. That 1962 model could reach 92 mph and was soon a target for Germany's embryonic tuning industry (especially Alpina) to release more power. However, it was the mechanically similar but enlarged 1.8-liter versions of 1,734 and 1,753 cc (as installed in the 1800 and derivatives), able to deliver up to 130 street horsepower (1800TI/SA) or 160 competition bhp, that attracted the most sporting attention after 1963. These later four-cylinders all had chain-driven overhead-camshaft layout and slant installations. BMW, however, ventured extensively into belt drive with the smaller M60 six-cylinders of the seventies (as sup-

How it was in the 02 beginning: the fuel-injected 2002Tii original of the 1970s in a bleak mid-winter Munich.

Picture: BMW Archiv Munich, 1971

plied for the E21 3 Series and the 5 Series from E12 onward) and the M42 four-cylinders of the 1980s 3 and 5 Series.

The 1500 also established production BMW basics such as front-engine, rear-drive: at press time, only the rare Baur-handbuilt mid-engine M1 has deviated from this layout. Other familiar technical features embrace MacPherson-strut front suspension and independent rear suspension through trailing arms. Today's BMWs have an unrecognizably reworked rear suspension that uses multiple links to provide class-leading traction and suspension behavior around trailing arms.

The sixties 1500 and many of its successors sported mixed disc/drum braking, along with worm-and-roller steering. It wasn't until the 1968 2500/2800 sedan series that rear discs were production-line regulars.

The 1500 was the most important BMW for traveling the road back to shiny black figures on the corporate bank account. It spawned a line of fleet four-cylinders that are now collector's legends, especially the 02 two-door sedans of 1966–75. Such 02 cousins took on previous four-door running gear and gave it new sporting life. For example, the twin-carburetor, 120-bhp four-cylinder developed for the 1800TI was faster, lighter and (not much) cheaper than its parents, as installed for the 1802.

American influence pushed BMW into the classic alliance of the 02 body with the 1,990-cc, 100-bhp, single-carburetor engine as the 2002. The 2002 then multiplied with its own stunning ferocity: we had the well-balanced 2002TI in LHD only, which offered 120 bhp and 115 mph, leading to the 2002Tii, the logical benchmark of European 2-liter performance sedans. This meant a 130-bhp power rush coupled to then-unheard-of economy for such a powerful 1,990-cc, because it featured Kugelfischer mechanical fuel injection.

Such success engendered an arrogant madness, so that BMW learned some painful lessons with the end-of-run 2002 turbo. It will always be listed in history as Europe's first turbo production car (pre-dating Porsche and Saab). Yet this non-intercooled 170-bhp powerhouse, with its stripy color scheme and reversed decaling (designed to be read in the mirror of the car about to be overtaken!), upset the political sensitivities of the time Europe was then stuck fast in a fuel crisis engendered by the 1973-74 winter repercussions of an Arab-Israeli war. Still, even ten years after it was made, it was fun to zip off 0–60 mph in seven seconds or less....

In our next chapter, we explore how a now-prospering BMW reinvented its prewar tradition for fabulous coupes, leading to the 1976–1989 life of the equally fabulous 6 Series.

QUICK FACTS

Period

1956-1975

Products

Big Bimmer coupes. Specifically 3200CS; 2000 C/ CS;
2800 CS; 3.0 CS/CSi ; three road variants of CSL and
all racing counterparts

Performance

From 100 to 800 bhp

Production

From outputs measured by the hundred in the fifties
and the early sixties, BMW Coupe production hit
44,237 in all the Karmann-bodied C to CSL
variants of the 1965-75 decade

The Big BMW Coupes

A legendary reputation for coupe excellence, based upon elegant speed coupled with collectible durability, preceded the debut of the 6 Series

BMW purists might opt for the pre World War II coachwork and coupes on the 328 chassis/running gear, wrought by specialists such as Wendler at Reutlinging, as the true beginning of a sporty 2-door BMW offering an extra sparkle from the style and exceptional performance. To the author's mind, a more realistic starting point to analyzing the sources for the 1976–89 6 Series can be found in the post-war car manufacturing activities of BMW at Munich, rather than the pre-war Eisenach operation.

Inevitably, we find an Italian in our list of styling sources. However, we also discovered a Paris-domiciled Frenchman, and a long retired BMW Chief Engineer, Bernhardt Osswald, who dominated the production engineering of BMW between 1965 and 1975.

There were many other influences upon the seductive 6 Series, but a key facet of the German market is a taste for 2-door coupes built over production sedan components. This allows the stylists full reign upon a practical and affordable foundation. There was even a two-door coupe derivative of the 30–40 horsepower flat twin 700. This 1959 Michelotti of Turin coupe predated the sedan derivative by a year.

However, it was with the larger BMW products that the BMW reputation for glamorous coupes was re-established in the fifties. The overtones of the American market were not lost on BMW in Germany, so that the success of the Ford Thunderbird and Chevrolet Corvette were taken as good omens for future lucrative export deals. Thus the Graf Goertz penned 503 and 507 carried strong transatlantic echoes during their 1956–1959 limited production lives.

The 328 was clothed in a number of aerody-namically-proven bod-ies in hand-curved aluminum. This is the 1939 Le Mans and 1940 Mille Miglia outline from Carozzeria Tour-ing, a winning coupe that could reach nearly 140 mph, thanks to an aero Cd factor of 0.35— a figure unbeaten by many designs of the late nineties!

Picture: BMW Mobile Tradition/Munich 1996

   Such rakish designs also allowed BMW's aluminum V8 another outlet. Much of the running gear previewed in the 501/502 sedans was to be found beneath the long bonnets and flowing lines of the 503 and 507, including the unique steering, gearbox and basic suspension. A 507's rear suspension was further modified from that mass production format, incorporating a Panhard rod and location links to resist the acceleration and top speed (118–137 mph, depending on rear drive ratio) harvested by the 160 horsepower eight.

   Although the 503 and 507 were very rare beasts, neither exceeding a production run of 500, the principle of the larger sporting BMW V8 did reach the sixties within the 3200CS Coupe. It was styled by Bertone and built on the same 2835 mm /111.6" wheelbase as a 503 (the 507 had been considerably shortened in this area). The 3200CS was significant, not for a then worthy 160 bhp at 5600 rpm, or for the twin Zenith 36 mm carbure-tors set up on the highest compression ever offered for the V8 (9:1), but for the body design.

In the public mind, Italy is associated with coupes, but BMW knows this niche better than anyone when it comes to profitable 2+2s, especially with six cylinders. Here, we see the M6/M635CSi with its family tree above. They are: the 2000C/CS, the 3200CS (the last BMW V8 coupe until 840i), and the rakish 327. The latter was a 55-horsepower six-cylinder, but the great-grandfather of the M6 was the 327/28, which saw the glorious 80-horsepower 328 engine implanted in those inspired lines.

Picture: BMW Archiv
Released 1998

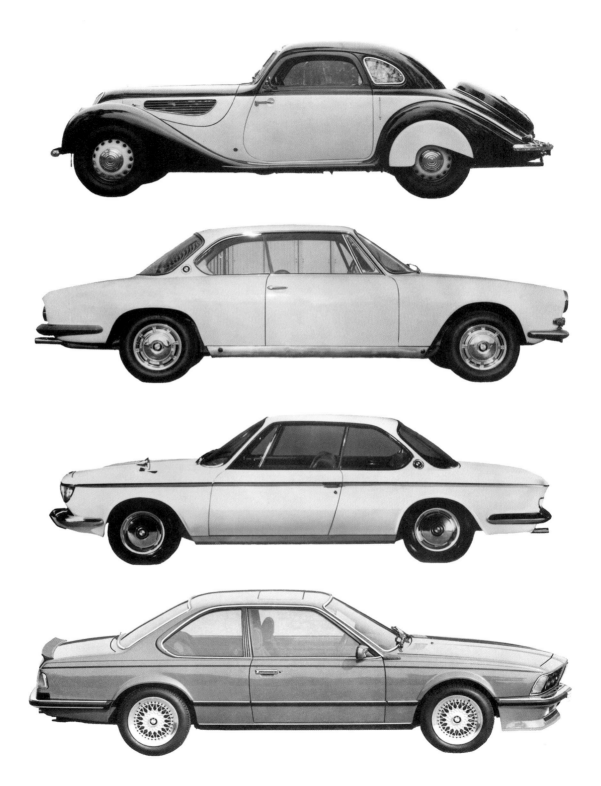

Another click of the photographic rewind button brings us this British-domiciled sport and coupe collection from BMW GB. They are (right to left): the right-hand-drive version of 328 (Frazer-Nash), the street-specification M1, an early engineering version of the 850i for UK type-approval development, a total CSL restoration, and the flowing lines of the 507. Since the picture was taken, both the 850 and the CSL have been sold, while the remainder work hard on publicity-related functions.

Picture: BMW GB 1989

As for the 1500 *Neue Klasse* four door, Munich enlisted the help of Bertone, Turin's oldest current coachbuilder. Founded in 1907 and run today by the son of the founder, Bertone in the late fifties and early sixties was home for a new major influence in Italian automotive haute couture: Giorgetto Giugiaro.

In 1959, at the age of 21, Giugiaro became the chief stylist at Bertone. This was a post about as influential on automotive design trends as becoming chief engineer at VW during the Golf's gestation into a Model T-challenging bestseller—one that would last four generations.

From 1959–65, Giugiaro's reign under the shrewd guidance of Nuccio Bertone produced over 20 serious prototype or production cars. Best known were the 1963 Alfa Romeo Giulia Sprint Coupe, and Fiat's 850 (later 903-engined) coupe, both of which were produced in considerable numbers and exerted a strong influence over later 'updates' of their basic lines, or coupes from rival manufacturers.

In the earliest days of his stay, Giugiaro and the Turin team drew the 3200 and had it manufactured in prototype trim. Originally they had both coupe and cabriolet (convertible) prototypes, but only the coupe was made - and then in the usual restricted volume.

The glamorous BMW 503 V8 cabriolet of the fifties shared its rugged frame chassis and aluminum V8 (albeit in lower-power trim) with the 507. BMW production figures released in the nineties indicated two primary batches of 503 manufacture, totaling 407 units.

Drawing: BMW
Released 1978

The significance to the eighties was in the creation of a large coupe with exceptionally uncluttered lines, an extraordinary amount of cabin glass, and the emphasis on the BMW family look that is basic in Munich's styling/marketing philosophy. For the 507, Graf Goertz had dared to drop the BMW *Nieren*, or kidney-style grille that had existed in one form or another since the thirties. Yet Bertone emphasized the tradition at the front and created that curved "hook" to the side rear window that runs throughout BMW models today, and the 6 Series was no exception. Look back and you can see the same "reverse dog leg" antithesis to fifties American front "windshield" pillar shapes, upon the similarly uncluttered panels of the 1500.

Only three BMW CS (Coupe Sport) were constructed in the Frankfurt show debut year of 1961. Just another 535 were made before production of the last V8 BMW from the first post-war generation was to cease in 1965. It would be almost thirty years before BMW created a new generation of V8s. The 3200CS was far more significant than the sum of its production run. The 3300 lb/124 mph coupe with its early (for BMW) use of front disc brakes was a surprisingly accurate preview of the aspirations BMW held to resume their role as purveyors of civilized and spacious coupes.

To replace the 3200CS, BMW reached further into their own resources. Although the end product was constructed by Karmann at Osnabruck, the

BMW Dingolfing facility, some 373 miles to the south, would take over manufacturing the 6 Series, after an initial spell with Karmann .

In June 1965, a new generation of BMW coupes—the 2000CS and 2000C—appeared on the German market. The single carburetor C and twin carburetor CS utilized unitary steel chassis construction, instead of the separate ladder chassis layout of 501–507 related sedans and coupes. The basic structure beneath the 2 liter running gear was that of the contemporary 1800 4-door, also made by Karmann at Osnabruck.

The cabin area of the C/CS featured acres of glass, and the inevitable side rear window "dog leg" to faithfully echo the Bertone-Giugiaro style. However, BMW's in-house specialist Wilhelm Hofmeister ensured that this coupe had a completely individual look, one that was always controversial. At the front it had wrap around headlamps for most markets (some British examples deployed quad lamps). At the back the lamps were superbly blended into the metalwork, a fashion that was to last BMW a full 10 years, as was the pillarless (again a Bertone echo) side glass treatment.

BMW was still firmly in the 4-cylinder era, and it must be said that the 2000 coupes did not earn universal gasps of admiration for their per-

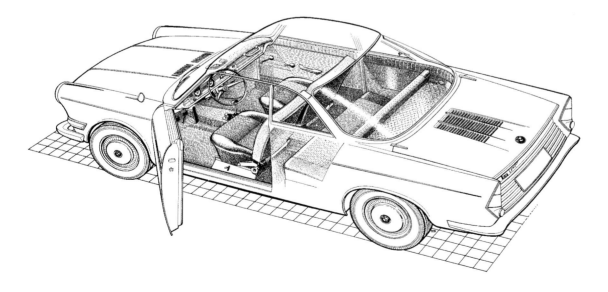

Inside the later BMW LS coupe, we can see that it grew to a reasonably accommodating 2+2 in the 1964–65 seasons. Some 1,475 coupes of various 700 series were exported to the US following batch manufacture in 1962, but the updated 700LS coupe was confined to Europe. Total manufacture of all 700 coupe types reached 27,181 in the period 1959–65. The rarities were the 413 units made in right-hand-drive for Britain.

Drawing: BMW Archiv
Original, 1964

The front-engine, rear-drive BMW layout is well displayed in this factory cutaway of the 2000C coupe. Back then, the front coil spring dampers were inclined forward, rather than slanted back in strut format. The engine had four cylinders, but the essentials (particularly the floorpan) provided a base for the next generation of six-cylinders in sizes from 2.5 to 3.2 liters.

Drawing: "SW" for BMW Munich Republished 1979

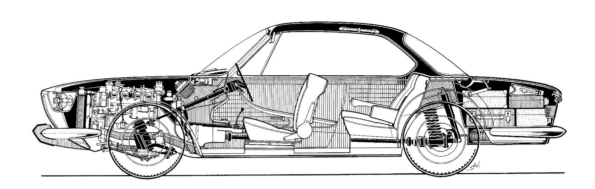

formance, which was inevitably less than the previous beefy 3.2 liter V8s. The 2000 (89 x 80 mm for 1990 cc), delivered 100 bhp with a single 40 mm Solex carburetor. Another 20 bhp was provided from the same capacity when twin 40mm side draft carburetors were installed alongside a 9.3:1 compression. These power figures were most familiar to the European public in the 2002 and 2002TI Series.

Within the 2640 lb (1200 kg) coupes, the single carburetor BMW power plant allowed a 107 mph maximum speed with 13 seconds required to plod the 2000C from rest to 62 mph. There was an automatic transmission option that was slower still and delivered just over 20 UK mpg. A twin carburetor 2000CS cheered post-65 performance levels a little: they quoted 0–62 mph in 12 seconds and a 115 mph maximum. Yet it was debatable whether the coupes were really any faster than the 1966–68 2000TI 4-door cousins, or the 1966–72 BMW 2000 sedan, this despite their overtly sporting heritage.

In fact BMW's hotshot of the period was the homologation racing sedan, 1800TI/SA ("Tisa"). Its 1964–5 limited run extracted 130 bhp at 6100 rpm from its 1773cc (84 x 80 mm) BMW/4-cylinder as the basis for European Championship winning performance. Complete with twin 45mm side draft carburetors the "Tisa" would launch from 0–60 mph in just 9 seconds and was the Bavarian reply to lightweight Alfa Romeo coupes and the Ford Mustang/Cortina assault on the European Touring Car Championship (ETCC).

Because the 2000C/CS coupes were built on the 1800 floorpan the company used the usual MacPherson strut front suspension and a trailing arm rear end, supported via a traditional mixed disc and drum brake sys-

A twenty-year contrast: the 1965–69 2000CS lines up below one of 1989's last model year M635CSi series in European trim, complete with color-coded wrap-around bumpers.

Pictures: BMW Archiv Munich Released 1989

tem. The 100.4 inch (2550 mm) wheelbase and front/rear track figures of 52.4 inches (1330 mm) and 54.2 inches (1375 mm) were also shared between 2000 coupes and the 1800 sedans, and the later 4-door 2000, for that matter.

The 2000 coupes were phased out in February 1970 after 13,691 examples had been manufactured, the CS proving most popular with a memorable 9,999 produced. By comparison, just 443 examples of the 2000C were created between May 1967 and September 1968, while the automatic accounted for 3,249 of the output.

From September 1968, it was public knowledge as to what BMW's coupe ambitions would be for the seventies. At that time, when the 6-cylinder BMW 2500 and 2800 sedans were announced, a 2800CS coupe cousin was being made at Karmann from December 1968. There was no 2500 counterpart coupe, until the 1974–5 fuel crisis forced the domestic market sale of a smaller engine model. Unlike the 2000C/CS, BMW statistics do reveal unique shipments of the 2800CS in American specification. Beginning August 1969 and terminating March 1971, some 1,167 were shipped to the US, the manual transmission model (641) proving marginally more popular.

The 2800CS, carrying perhaps the sweetest 6-cylinder engine of the original "Big 6" generation, began a BMW coupe legend that would be hard for any successor to emulate. In retrospect this was slightly surprising, as the 2800CS was far from a thoroughbred.

Although BMW had developed their family look with extraordinary success, so that the coupe and sedan 2800 were clearly on kissing cousin terms, appearances were extremely deceptive. The 2800CS used a revitalized version of 2-litre Karmann coupe bodywork, rather than the foundations of the more recent 6-cylinder sedans. Similar illusions were later used to publicly tie together 6 and 7 Series in the late seventies and mid-eighties, yet the basic 6 Series floorpan was that of the 5 Series, instead of the visually similar 7 Series.

Inserting the 6-cylinder engine in what amounted to a 2000 coupe (from the windshield pillar rearward) involved a substantial, and beneficial, redesign. Overall length went from 178.3 inches (4530 mm) to 182.3 inches (4630 mm), most of that extra four inches devoted to wrenching in the still 30 degree slant six cylinder engine block. Wheelbase and track were also increased compared to the 2-litre coupes. The 2800 CS rode on a wheelbase of 103.4 inches (2625mm), a three inch stretch of the original. It had a front/rear track measurement of 56.9 inches (1446 mm) and 55.1 inches (1402 mm), that near five inch front expansion reflecting the installation of the six cylinder car's front struts and disc brakes, along with

6J x 14 steel wheels in initial German production. At the rear the 2800CS continued with the 9.8 in (250 mm) rear drum brakes which traced back to the 1500, the 10.7 inch (272 mm) discs of the usual non-ventilated type of the period, and also familiar in other BMW applications.

The 6-cylinder 2800CS naturally displayed a weight gain to a hefty 2981 lb (1355 kg), but it was more than offset by the power of the 86 x 80 mm twin down draft Zenith carbureted 2788 cc. At 6000 rpm there was another 50 hp (170 total) available from the engine, and that was accompanied by a substantial 172 lb-ft of torque at 3700 rpm.

Enough to carry that big two door coupe toward 130 mph—the factory recorded 128 mph; *Motor* magazine confirmed exactly that figure. The factory only reckoned on 10 seconds for 0–62 mph, but that was overly modest; *Motor* made it 8.5 seconds for 0–60 mph and many others concurred.

Anywhere around 20mpg was typical for hard-driven 2.8 liter coupes, the factory, their usual pessimistic selves, forecasting 17.1 mpg, which was more likely for the slower automatic. Anywhere from 19–23 mpg over British terrain appeared normal.

The carbureted 2.8 sold nearly the same total as both 2000C/CS had managed, exactly 9399 in its three season life, before it followed the sedans up the enlarged engine (three liter) path in 1971. Just as important as the 89 x 80 mm (*née* 2-litre four) dimensions for 2985cc and an extra 10hp (180 bhp at 6000 rpm), was the adoption of 4-wheel 10.7 in (272 mm) ventilated disc brakes.

The chassis behavior of the 2800CS was usually criticized for an inferiority when compared to contemporary BMW sedans—which were built from scratch rather than converted designs, as had been the coupe case. Given the capability of those disc brakes, and the sheer speed of 3.0 CS, it was nice to be able to slow before things got completely out of hand...

As the 2800CS had not been available in the UK until October 1969, it was not surprising to find that the 1971—introduced 3.0CS, as discussed, and its fuel-injection (Bosch D-Jetronic) brother of 1971 took until January 1972 and May of the same year (3.0CSi) to permeate the UK.

The 3.0CSi with its slightly uprated 9.1:1 compression ratio, instead of the usual 9:1 ratio, plus the fuel injection equipment, was rated with 200 bhp at 5500 rpm, thus saving 500 rpm over the carbureted coupe's power peak. Also a meaty 200 lb-ft of torque at 4300 rpm was available, versus the 3.0CS on 188 lb-ft at 3700 rpm.

The 3.0Si/CSi was a quick car in sedan or coupe style: BMW reported 136 mph and 0-62 mph in 8 seconds. Independent road testers discovered that the 3.0CSi ran out of steam at just over 130 mph, but there were a few who managed high 7-second acceleration times at 0–60 mph in the UK. Fuel consumption hovered around the 16 mpg mark (20 UK mpg), if the car was driven with restraint; harsher use recorded some 13–14 mpg (16–17 UK mpg) overall.

The 3.0CS/CSi coupes were made from April 1971 to November 1975 with a total of 20,051 constructed, excluding 1,039 CS/CSi that were utilized in the *Motorsport*-related homologation process described later.

However, it was not the commercially-durable 3.0 CS/CSi machines of 1971–75 that attracted most public attention, or that ensured the expensive interest of collectors in the early seventies BMW coupes. No, public attention was directed at a new big BMW coupe, one that peeked its limited production nose into a LHD-only world during 1971. To further their European sedan car racing priorities, BMW made many coupe performance moves in the 1971–73 period. Priority one was the CSL, L for *leichtgewicht,* the German equivalent of lightweight. Lower curb weight was achieved by a wide use of alloy panels, fragile on the street, but brilliant for boosting power to weight ratios.

Awesome Armada. Hans Stuck—who was back on the BMW driving strength at Le Mans 1998—heads his CSL teammate in one of the 1973-season CSL coupes in the British round of the European season. Alpina-BMW won the event, but you can see why it was so hard for the Six to replace the charismatic seventiess BMW coupes of the CS to CSL series.

Picture: LAT/Silverstone, UK 1973

Prototype CSLs were seen in 1971 Germany, but they were not homologated in time to make the difference to BMW racing fortunes for 1972. Then BMW also acquired the Ford Cologne personnel who were driving forces behind the Ford Capri's success in lightweight, fuel injection, V6 specification. Key was former Cologne Competitions Manager and ex-Porsche Team driver Jochen Neerpasch, who oversaw the development of BMW Motorsport GmbH. Neerpasch was supported in everything outside Paul Rosche's traditional engine responsibilities by the engineering expertise of Martin Braungart, who was another Ford refugee bored by their domination of the sedan racing world.

The managerial duo brought with them, from 1973 onward, Hans Joachim Stuck, who became the archetypal BMW racer of the seventies and early eighties. H.J. Stuck senior was the German Grand Prix and hill climbing legend for Auto Union and when Junior left BMW in the eighties he served much of his competition career with either Audi or Porsche. The other driving name that US and European spectators always associated with BMW was that of Austrian Dieter Quester, who was Alexander Von Falkenhausen's son-in-law and four time winner of the European sedan title, including a victory achieved in a 635CSi.

Another key name in our story has present day corporate American links. Back in 1971, Bob Lutz led BMW's marketing men and his sporting ambition began another significant strand of the BMW reputation for fast coupe motoring.

The CSL started as a lighter CS in September 1972 to June 1973 production, over which time just 1039 examples were manufactured, half of them (500) to a unique RHD, heavier UK specification. All of the lightweight CS coupes shared the usual carburetored 2985 cc six, rated at 180bhp. The lightweight panels included easily scarred doors, hood, and trunk lids. Other weight savers were special seats, sports steering wheel, and 7J x 14 inch alloy wheels with 195.70VR radial tires. I drove such a car for *Motor Sport* magazine in July 1972 and that was much more in the spirit of stripped-out performance than the subsequent 500-off run of more luxuriously equipped (with the majority of lightweight panels) CSLs sold (often at discount) in the UK.

Quoted weight for a 3.0CS rose to 3080 lbs (1400 kg), while the CSL was credited with 440 lbs (200 kg) less. In road terms that was worth a complete second from the official 0–62 mph acceleration time, plus a mysteriously gained 2 mph for an official maximum of 134 mph.

Neerpasch and his ex-Ford colleagues arrived at Munich and started lighting fires under the backsides of BMW performance specialists Alpina and Schnitzer with hefty cash bonus schemes. BMW Motorsport GmbH quickened the pace of large coupe competition development so that the CSL format became critical.

The second stage in CSL development was a slightly oversize (3003 cc) version of the fuel-injected six that differed from the 2985 cc sextet only in the provision of a 0.25 mm bonus in the cylinder bores, yielding an official 89.25 x 80 mm. Power, some 200 bhp and the 9.5:1 compression with 201 lb-ft of torque, were left as before.

Weight for the evolutionary 3.0CSL had risen 140 lbs. (70 kg) to a total 2794 lbs (1270 kg). However, the sole purpose of this model was to ensure that BMW could race with an engine capacity beyond 3-liters, whereas the rival Fords were stuck with using engines beneath 3-liters.

BMW Motorsport began the 1973 racing season with a 3191 cc 6-cylinder variant (92 x 80 mm), a stretch that was race-tuned by Paul Rosche and his M-Team to deliver 340 bhp at 7800 rpm. This accessible power was more than the Ford/Weslake V6 in the Capri could deliver after years of development. Even Ford's use of unique alloy Weslake cylinder heads, patterned on the company's speed equipment for the ex-Mustang/GT40 Ford 289 V8, failed to close the power deficiency to BMW.

For 1973, the BMWs still operated at a considerable racing weight disadvantage, for the Ford was homologated for International Competition at under 2000 lbs (1000 kg). BMW countered with a yet larger version of its fabled six, one that utilized the 94 mm bore, proving that a 93.4 mm bore was a safe mass production figure for the later M1 and early 635 CSi road cars.

The Kugelfischer fuel-injected unit measured 3.3 liters (94 x 80 mm), operated at 11.2:1 compression and served up a beefy 366 bhp x 8200 rpm. Paul Rosche and the M-Team wanted more, more cubic capacity, more power—but that was a minor part of the CSL tale in its final form.

Engineer Martin Braungart (cofounder of the BBS Wheel concern) and a few trusted colleagues produced a fantastic multiple-piece aerodynamic wing for the racing CSL. Recognized for racing from July 1,1973, the homologation process mandated that a series of showroom CSLs had to be produced around such key racing additions.

The showroom six (89.25 mm bore x 84 mm stroke) was officially uprated to yield 206 bhp at 5600 rpm from 3153 cc. Pulling power was also improved, not that this was a notable deficit in any big BMW 6; maximum torque was reported at 211 lb-ft at 4200 rpm. Such road cars were rated as capable of 138 mph without the wings and 140 mph (wings installed) with 0–60 mph quoted in 7 seconds flat.

The subsequently dominant racing CSL was bored to a then daring 94 x 84mm (3496 cc) and would provide 370 bhp at 8000 rpm some 200 rpm less than its 3.3 liter predecessor. Although initially distrusted, the 3.5 liter unit certainly helped to win races against Fords that were rather optimistically rated at little more than 320/330 bhp on half a liter less. However, it was BMW's "Batmobile" wing system that demoralized the opposition.

Braungart and Co. created a deep front spoiler to be used in alliance with front bonnet strakes, a hoop over the rear window, plus an enormous rear wing. This was supported by two vertical blades on the road car, but was developed for competition with triple pylons to defeat any wing flutter at the CSL's 170 mph gait. Beneath the rear wing, it was easy to overlook a conventional spoiler lip that edged the trunk of the CSL, and was often the only rear aerodynamic device to be seen in the showroom.

Braungart confided that the front and rear air dams/spoilers, plus that rear wing, were the vital components. They provided such downforce that BMW Motorsport frequently ran softer compound competition tires than the opposition, with consequent high-G benefits.

Ford Management had dickered about to such a degree that the Capris' racing requirements had been casually neglected. The Capri faced the racing CSL with just a front spoiler; not even a "duck-tail" was homologated for the racing Ford's trunk-lid until 1974.

The effect of BMW's rapidly-developed aerodynamic ability was cruelly brought home to Ford at the July 1973 Nürburgring 6 Hours. Both Ford and BMW depended on all the Grand Prix names they could find, although Alpina-BMW had the best prospect in subsequent triple World Champion Niki Lauda.

Now a familiar sight on the Ferrari pit wall, Lauda pulled out pole position for the Alpina CSL in that summer of 1973. Niki set a benchmark 8 minutes 17.3 seconds versus 8 minutes 23 seconds for the fastest Ford around Nürburgring's legendary 14 mile North circuit.

Despite Ford using the talent of triple World Champion Jackie Stewart and double World/Indycar Champion Emerson Fittipaldi, BMW swept the board at Nurburgring, and Ford failed to win another European Championship round for the remainder of 1973.

The CSL's official production life lasted until late 1975, but it lived on as a competitive racing sedan in Group 2 and Group 5 long after its production demise. Unusually, even the factory ran the obsolete CSL in 1976, while privateers carried on with the 3.5 racing motor and the full wing kit to win every European Touring Car Championship title until 1979. A truly magnificent old warrior!

The racing CSL was extremely popular and a great attraction for spectators. It set new standards of racing success for BMW, and it occasionally beat the obviously more suitable rear-engined Porsche 911 when campaigned in the 1976 Group 5 World Championship.

Work had started on a 24 valve (M49 coded) 6-cylinder racing motor in September 1973, and it is this unit which subsequently inspired the motivation of both M1 [coded M88] and the S38-engined M6 coupe. In racing format, over 400 bhp was immediately provided by the 3.2 liter M49 prototype.

Despite the Arab/Israeli 1973–74 fuel crisis slashing race budgets in Europe, the 24 valve unit debuted in a pair of CSLs for the 1974 Austrian European Championship Round at Salzburgring. Hans Joachim Stuck/ Jacky Ickx hurtled to a win over class Ford opposition with M-power of 440bhp at an inspired 8500 rpm.

For subsequent American (1975) and Group 5 (1976 onward) use, the M49 was redeveloped in the Winter of 1975–6 to yield a reliable 470 bhp at 9000 rpm. Josef Schnitzer had the bright idea of mounting the straight six vertically, instead of the usual production 30 degree slant, and new water channeling combated overheating, while the upright stance also allowed the exhaust manifolds a power-boosting, straighter run.

Coupe lineage stretches through 02s to the 3-series (21 and E30), from the 700LS of the sixties to the 1992 E36 3-series range. The 3-series BMW coupe line of the nineties, with either four- or six-cylinder power, was a regular bestseller in its sector in Europe.

Picture: BMW/Munich, Ismaning, 1992

The full advantage of mounting the 6-cylinder vertically became apparent in 1976, when BMW supported the efforts of three well-financed teams in Group 5 CSLs to take on Porsche, and BMW also fielded their own development car.

This was the ultimate CSL. Coded M49/4, the twin-cam motor thundered forth 750/800 bhp from 3191 cc and was equipped with two KKK turbo-chargers. The monster CSL raced only three times, remembered best in the hands of the late Ronnie Peterson, but it was the most sensational sedan a manufacturer has yet dared to officially create. It had the ability to fry the drivers' feet, and produce wheel-spin in 3rd gear, well beyond 100 mph, all with long licks of flame to delight spectators during its (usually) brief appearances.

While the Turbo did not lead to any great affection at BMW for the production of Turbo cars—only the 2002 and 745i have entered BMW production as gasoline powered vehicles—the quad-valve 6-cylinder has become critical to BMW's showroom product. This is particularly true of BMW performance coupes from the M6 onward to the M3.

Meanwhile, the remaining production output of CSLs were officially 3.2 liter coupes, using the 3153 cc/206 bhp unit discussed earlier. For the road there were neat spats to extend the wheel-arches, rather than the huge fenders favored by the racers. The standard showroom wheel remained a 7J x 14" alloy with 195/70 VR tires usually sourced from Michelin. The later CSLs (57 were made from June 1974 to November 1975) had upgraded interiors with sports front seats, a more sporting steering wheel, and little else to define their collectable status.

The issue of CSL road cars is complicated by the fact that three engine sizes were officially fitted (2985, 3003, and 3153 cc) in at least as many trim variations. For example alloy skinned door panels would appear to be a must for any CS carrying the L-designation, but the British specification omitted these fragile door skins and added a number of luxury items. A casual look at the pristine example operated by Tim Hignett of L & C BMW in Southern Britain showed electric rear side window operation and the resolute use of many steel external panels.

Better known was the fact that the 3.2 CSL could not be sold in its home market with the wing kit installed, because such aerodynamic additions were not homologated for road use in Germany or Switzerland. The wing set was dutifully placed in the trunk, and could then be retrofitted by the first owner. A similarly effective wing kit, delivered to proud owners in the trunk, was also a feature of the 1994 Alfa Romeo Silverstones that dominated the British Touring Car Championship. There are no original automotive engineering ideas left!

BMW's big CSi/CSL coupes remained in production until November 1975, and officially totaled 21,147 examples in their four year span. More relevant to the subsequent 6 Series might be the total production figure from the September 1965 debut of the 2000C to the November 1975 termination of CSi/CSL at an aggregate 44,237 coupes. It would be a hard act to follow, but BMW designers and engineers were assigned the task of creating the 6 Series to do just that.

QUICK FACTS

Period

1974–89

Products

Previous CS (E9 to E24-coded) 6 Series
design parameters

People

Designer Paul Bracq, engineer Bernhard
Osswald, US importer Max Hoffman

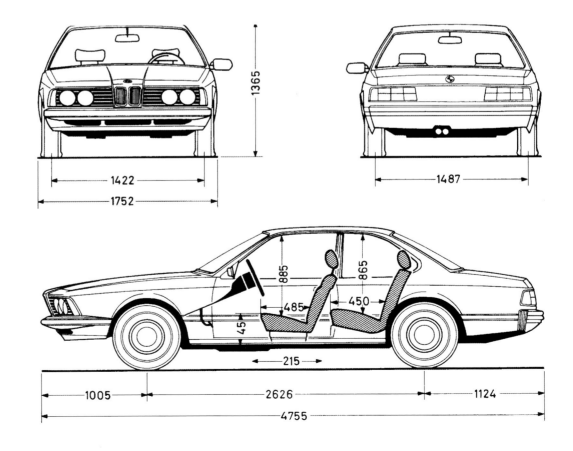

Conception of a Coupe Classic

American market strength, as well as a French stylist, shaped the embryonic 6 Series

As the seventies began, a number of widely differing influences within BMW molded the final form of the 6 Series coupes. The most obvious inputs for a vehicle that many saw as BMW's flagship were those of Parisian design and styling chief Paul Bracq, and the practical engineering output of BMW's top technocrat in 1965–75, Bernhard Osswald. However, there were some more subtle market forces to take into account as well.

We must also acknowledge the disruption to neatly laid marketing plans of the 1973–74 fuel crisis in Europe (and the later seventies fuel queues in the US) and the politics surrounding importation of BMWs into the US.

Austrian Max Hoffman, the vigorous US importer, had always attracted controversy. What no auto enthusiast could take away from Hoffman was that he encouraged sporty specials such as the 1800 TI/SA in the unique American street and sports worlds of the early sixties. Then Hoffman sparked the mating of 2-litres and the 02 shell to create the apparently immortal appeal of the 2002 in the later sixties.

However, it was not a surprise when BMW took control of their American outlet, because there had been vociferous criticism of the way the marque was handled in the US, and the after-sales treatment of customers. After legal battles with the voluble Hoffman, BMW took over in 1975 and renamed the import operation BMW North America.

Since 1950 Hoffman had imported increasing numbers of BMWs into America (some 13,700 in 1973), but there was always room to sell more in the land of opportunity. In less than three years, BMW NA sold close to

30,000 units to double sales and they exceeded 52,000 in 1982. Today BMW sales regularly exceed 100,000 units annually.

Thus America had become BMW's prime export market—a position it holds today with roughly double the sales of a major market like the UK—and its consumer demands had to be an integral component in the planning of any new BMW, especially a luxury coupe of particularly American market appeal.

From a practical engineering stance, BMW's facilities were constantly improving, although they lacked their own wind tunnel during the gestation of the 6 Series. Which might just be the reason why all BMW's were so square-rigged through the eighties, long after Audi and Mercedes rivals had plumped for aerodynamic outlines.

Fresh, but family—that was the face incorporated on the 1976 European 630CS and 633CSi models when they debuted in 1976. The company promise for its latest in a long line of coupes was that it "...represents the best way a factory automobile can be brought in line with the abilities of its drivers."

Picture: BMW Munich/ Spain, 1976

Key dimensions in millimeters were all listed in these factory drawings, which reveal a wheelbase it shared with the contemporary 5 Series and a rear track that was 65 mm/ 2.6 inches wider than that of the front.

Drawing: BMW Munich, 1976/Supplied via BMW Archiv, 1998

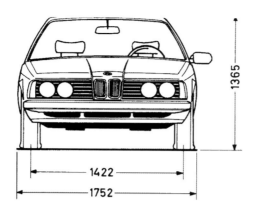

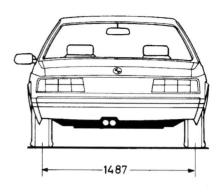

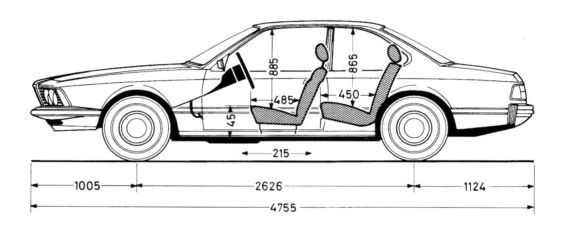

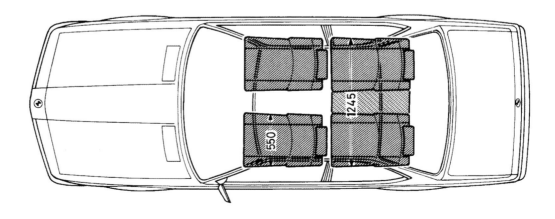

The fuel-injected six-cylinder 633CSi offered 200 bhp in a body that was a bit weightier than its equally powerful predecessors. As for so many BMWs following famous ancestors, one of the hardest engineering tasks was to inject excitement while vastly improving cabin, refinement, and safety.

Drawing: Niedermeier, BMW/Commissioned 1975, republished 1979

By 1975 BMW had opened their proving ground at Ismaning (stark reminders of the Dachau death camp loom at its fringes) on the Northern edge of Munich. Ismaning played a distinct role in improving the power slide safety aspects of BMW's then traditional oversteer handling characteristics, allowing the engineers to constantly test at the limit, safely away from the public. Contemporary reports reflected that the 6 Series was always seen as an exceptionally well-mannered and enjoyable drive. It's quite reassuring to know that safety was also a prime reason why the 6 Series weighed so much in its initial outline.

American legislation was incorporated in the thinking of the 6 Series at the development stage, a consideration which also applied at Jaguar of Coventry as they struggled to provide a credible successor to the E-type. Both companies had to replace well-loved designs with machines that were notably less elegant as all industry experts were confused by American demands. Tragically, in the case of Jaguar, this led to the abandonment of convertibles for many years, on the basis that they would never pass American roll-over crash test demands. This is also the reason that BMW was not to make another pillarless coupe to succeed the CS breed.

American regulations and market tastes were thus at the heart of BMW's design process for the CSi successor. The 6 Series design would be manufactured by BMW from 1976–1989, totaling over 86,000 and almost doubling the previous 2000C to 3.0CSi output by some 41,000. So you could say it was a success, commercially and competitively.

Most relevant of the American laws to affect 6 Series were those governing crash-testing, especially the inverted drop that probed roof crush-resistance. Such tests had already impacted on BMW thinking for the future 'Sixer'. For the 1974 model year and later, the CS grew grotesque big bumpers to meet Federal regulations. An American 3.0 CS or CSi weighed in at 3275 lb—in its sad final format—it was extended to 190 inches for the US, rather than the original figures of 2985 lb and 183.5 inches! Gross...

Legal battling with Max Hoffman formed a backdrop just when the previous series of 6-cylinder coupes (3.0 CSi) were ending their production lives at the Karmann and BMW assembly plants. So it was a particularly tricky moment for 6 Series to debut in the US. In fact the 3.0 CSi for the States had its sales life lengthened, selling into the 1976 model year even though Federal US CSi production ceased (according to nineties

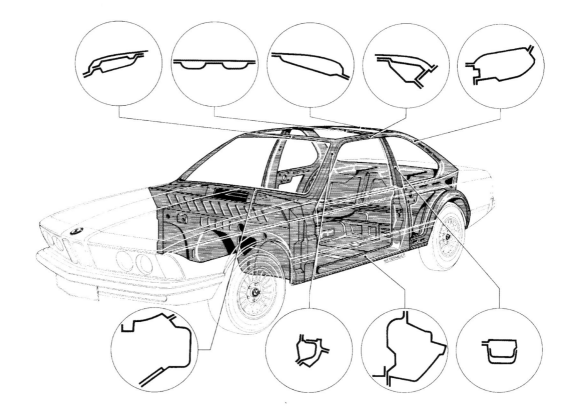

Here, you can see where so much of the 6 Series's weight gain occurred over its predecessors. Its body detail engineering was geared to American regulations, improving impact protection. It met rollover safety legislation in a way that would have been impossible with the traditional pillarless coupe design of earlier BMWs.

Drawing: Niedermeier, BMW/Courtesy BMW Archiv, 1998

There was the temptation to evolve more radical designs than the traditional front-engine, rear-drive format would permit. The M1 was a BMW rarity (only 450 made), but was an amiable, entirely practical, and exciting drive: one that could have been developed to compete commercially with the Porsche 911.

Picture: BMW Werkfoto, 1979

BMW records) in December 1974! Thus the 6 Series did not debut in the US until 1977, but we get ahead of ourselves...

BMW knew when styling a successor to the sixties-inspired coupes that any new design could not have the elegantly slim roof pillars and pillarless profile that BMW had made their own hallmark amongst desirable coupes. Paul Bracq's concern, carried out with sophistication in production, was to disguise the considerable structure needed to support the roof in such Federal tests.

There was also the sensible proviso that sufficient strength must be engineered into the structure to pass any future legislation—like Jaguar, BMW did not feel American crash standards would become anything other than harder to meet, and this meant some traditional cues had to be avoided.

According to BMW official literature, "this is the first coupe from Munich to have a central roof column". That does not mean 6 Series was the first BMW coupe with a formal B-pillar, for the pre-war designs from coachbuilders did have this feature, but it was certainly first mass production postwar 2-door to put safety over style.

Such considerations led BMW into a 6 Series that was necessarily beefier than its predecessors, as the frontal impact zones and crumple zone behavior (front and rear) demanded much more development time and the provision of, "a little more sheet metal than we would use today. In fact some of that extra weight was taken out of the later 6 Series," according to a very senior BMW engineering figure, speaking to the author in Munich, 1984.

Being chief stylist at BMW has never been an easy job, particularly for foreigners, as we can see from the comparatively brief tenures of Paul Bracq and subsequent eighties BMW recruit Martin Smith, the Briton who very swiftly went back to Audi.

What BMW means to Germans (especially Bavarians), and what it stands for in some export markets, differs. The designer has to walk a tightrope between imaginative vision and family values, echoes of other models in the range, or the now much more popular Retro look. As the natural desire of designers is to explore futuristic ideas, and do their absolute best to bring the future to today's consumer, this leads many newcomers into dispute at BMW.

BMW, like Mercedes and Porsche, carefully cultivated their core values in the seventies and eighties. They went for generally conservative style evolutions in the days when Six was conceived—back then a prod-

Dash successfully called on BMW's design credentials for clarity and ergonomic flair. Note the innovative 8-button test board to the left of the instrumentation and the four-spoke steering wheel with horn buttons in each spoke.

Drawing: Niedermeier, BMW

Detail design within was superb, as these highlights of the mirror power controls and molded rear headrest display. The sections behind both rear head supports lift to reveal the speakers and small, carpeted storage for valuables. Also visible is the roller blind for the back window—be warned that the plastic retaining hooks can get brittle and snap, especially in cool climates.

Pictures: BMW Werkfoto, 1987

uct like the Mercedes A-class front driver would have been regarded as
the devil's spawn. Even the hint that an American-made BMW could
succeed would have sent the Bavarian workforce into an unremitting
cycle of fear and loathing.

Paul Bracq rendered his 1972 vision of BMW's future in the creation of
a mid-engine, gullwing coupe with a distinct wedge theme. The 2-litre
turbo prototype was a popular motor show number and had the practical
appeal of deformable panels that would regain their shape following low
speed impacts. The BMW Turbo prototype proved a crowd-stopper at the
Autumn 1972 round of major auto shows, so a second example was fabricated around the transverse 4-cylinder power-train at Michelotti in Italy.

BMW retained the first example at their Munich museum and there is
no doubt that it was influential far beyond its exotic appearance—the
sloping nose still capacious enough to hold the traditional grille and the
hood/ nose sculptured around a raised center section that transferred over
to many subsequent Bimmers, including the Six.

The primary purpose of the car was to show that traditional BMW values could still be expressed in a radical 2-seater, a theme that had most

practical effect on the M1 as well as BMW self-confidence to blaze the Z1/ Z3 production trails.

At the April 1976 press debut of the E24-coded successors to the original E9 coupes (European 630CS and 633CSi), BMW acknowledged, " when designing the bodywork of this car, BMW followed along the lines of the Turbo design study, as can be seen at first sight. In fact, the typical front section with the inevitable BMW 'kid' (their way of translating kidney, not mine—JW) as well as the wedge-shaped body, which makes the car look as if it is going to jump to action any minute, has been accentuated with particular clarity with the new coupe."

General coupe themes of the period, such as a comparatively long bonnet and generous glass areas, were blended with traditional BMW themes such as the kidney grille and rear window "hook" outline. The quadruple headlamps were then a consistent BMW top model trademark, but the clever design team had also thought to firmly tie both front and rear end styling of the larger Six to a 7 Series debutante of 1977, delivered a year after Six. When the 6 Series was facelifted in the eighties, it also shared the softer front end appearance of the 7 Series, although—as we shall see— the pair were actually built on very different foundations.

The cold statistics were unusually revealing to guide us on the 6 Series role within the BMW range of 1976–89. Despite being built on the same wheelbase (103.3 inches) as its E9 predecessors, the E24 coupes were totally new and considerably larger and heavier. This was particularly true in the US where average figures showed the 6 Series up three inches in height and width, plus more than six inches added to the length; curb weight was up 350 lb.

No wonder there were performance criticisms of the replacement BMW coupe in the States, for engine power also dropped (in the worst case introductory years, from 3.0CSi's 200 bhp to 176 of 630CSi).

Yet there was some good news among the statistics to underline that BMW had made significant progress in the basic body design of 6 Series. The E9 CS/CSi generation had been ferocious beauties, stunners that evolved from an era when safety meant thinking about standard seat belt anchor points on the production line.

In contrast, note that any 6 Series is based on a scientifically crash-tested and developed automobile, braced by nine separate systems. These included a roll-over hoop, a crossmember behind the instrument panel and specific reinforcement (suggested by crash test analysis) to the upper windshield, rear screen, aft of the rear seats (underneath the package shelf) and "rigid longitudinal supports."

This reassuring safety factor is emphasized by a set of BMW percentages. When compared with its classic forebears, the 6 Series offered a massive 69 percent gain in torsional strength, 31 percent bonus in resistance "to shear forces" and was equipped with a near quarter (23 percent) enhanced frontal crumple zone. All achieved despite an increase of 7 percent in total glass areas.

When this was written, I had completed my first thousand miles in the first 6 Series I had driven since the eighties, and found that the interior appointments of the Six were one big benefit over its predecessors. Everything was made to far higher standards of rigidity, rounded off for safety and superbly constructed. My 12 year-old example has not had the interior renovated, but it is still in better condition after 87,000 miles than my wife's four year old Alfa on half those miles.

QUICK FACTS

Period

1972–1984

Products

BMW badging explained, plus 5 and 7 Series
component sources for 6 Series, and the
development of engines for American
and Europe

People

Walter Stork (chassis) and Georg Ederer
(power-train), plus badge lore
on a Trivial Pursuit scale

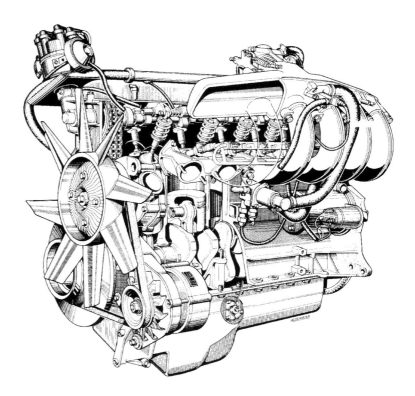

Hardware: Origins and Redevelopment

The 6 Series was the sum of many parts, usually taken from other BMW model ranges and given a new sporting twist. We detail the components, and the engineering behind their coupe applications

Any 6 Series coupe owed much to the 5 Series saloons. As direct replacements for the 4-door *Neue Klasse* 1800/2000 line of the sixties, they put BMW back on the road to prosperity. The 520 and its succession of multiple engine choice descendants also pioneered the logical cockpit layout, one that has been such a key element to making so many drivers feel right at home in any BMW. And the 5 Series also allowed the rebirth of the company's late thirties logic in the numbering system that badges each model

What's in a name?

To take the 520 as an example, the "5" prefix denotes the model series: at press time BMW had four major lines: 3, 5, 7, and 8 Series, plus specialist Z and M-prefixed models.

Usually, the secondary figures refer to the capacity in liters, so a 520 is a 2liter (122.1 cubic inches) and the 6 Series we discuss ascended from 628 to 635, some 2.8 to 3.5 liters (170.9 ci to 213.6 ci). In the case of the Z and M sub-species, number information is confined simply to the model line on which Z (sports 2-seaters) or M (for Motorsport) variants have been based.

Suffixes were added as the post-520 models switched to fuel injection (i). Specifically for 6 Series, you need to know the previous E9—and earlier—habit of labeling coupes following the logic of C for coupe, succeeded by S for sport. In the sixties a 2000CS meant that this variant had a twin carburetor engine offering 20 bhp more than a 2000C. When twin choke carburetors became routine, as for the CS application, fuel injection added the small "i". So that the majority of the product that we deal with here—and all the 6 Series that were officially imported to the US—carried the CSi suffix, unless...

BMW also developed a number of specialty lines and these could demand a letter prefix. Best known for Sixers is the M for Motorsport badge, which does not mean that the model concerned is a race car of some sort. That was the original intention, as for M1 and M3, but the 5 Series broke the mold with such commercial success that M-made is used for models that have no competition aspirations today.

For the 6 Series the M-prefix denoted the presence of a magnificent Motorsport co-engineered 24-valve engine, a direct descendant of the M1 motor. It offered a 68 bhp bonus over the single camshaft, 12-valve sixes of 635CSi, but unfortunately was never used in a motorsport application.

In Europe, these coupes were labeled M635CSi, but for the States the simpler and more prestigious M6 tag was applied (logical in view of M5 and subsequent M3). Unfortunately any official US import also suffered at the hands of Federal legislators and dropped 30 horsepower, from Europe's 286 bhp to America's 256 ponies.

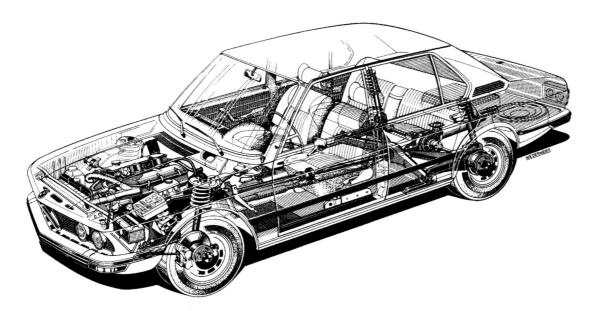

Major supplier: the original E12 BMW 5 Series (1974–81) and subsequent E28 (1981–88) provided much of the rugged running gear which sat beneath the Six's seductive lines. Initially, power units were drawn only from the 7 Series slant-six lines. Later, the 5 Series shared both 12- and 24-valve 3.5- and 3.4liter sixes that were otherwise reserved for the 6 Series of the 1980s.

Drawing: Niedermeier
BMW AG, 1974

Back when you could (mostly) believe what was badged on a BMW rump, we see the factory three-quarter rear illustrations for two very different coupes: the first generation 1978 635CSi (with a solid black rubber rear spoiler that was never specified in the US) and an M-designated 635CSi with the factory body-kit panels and the usual post-1987 blade rear spoiler.

Pictures: BMW Werkfotos, issued 1978 and 1998

Also exclusively badged for North America was the 1987 model year L-prefixed 635. This simply meant the traditional 635 single cam six and automatic transmission power train, designed to stand out against the M6 24-valve, manual 5-speed sporting option. The L6 was a slow seller, so the factory went back to the 635CSi in 1988, and examples were sold right through to 1992 even though the 850 had officially replaced the 6 Series in 1990 America.

Game for more badge lore?

There were two examples of 6 Series having changed engine capacity, but staying with a respected badge. For instance, post-summer 1982 downsizing of the straight six should have brought a 634 badge in place of 635; an American spec 633 should actually be a 632, because it shared a 3.2 liter motovation with a 7 Series, which was truthfully badged 732i in Europe but 733i throughout its US life!

BMW also broke their own rules when it came to the turbocharged 3.2 liter '745i.' Working on the basis that it made horsepower like a bigger engine, BMW used the international motor factor for turbocharging (x 1.4) to arrive at the 4.5 liter equivalent. BMW did not subsequently alter the figure when the big turbo was asked to generate the same 256 bhp in association with a more accessible torque from 3.5 liters.

Enough of the badges, let's talk hardware. A superb 6 Series interior came from BMW Design: it was generated in the wake of that 5 Series inspiration, the single pane viewing panel for a simple four dial layout in black and white.

Widely imitated in the seventies and eighties, the overall 5 Series cockpit theme was only mildly modified for the first generations of the 6 Series. It was then overhauled for the eighties 6 Series with a three spoke steering wheel to replace a dished four-spoke and revised central controls.

At that time, heating and ventilation temperatures, direction and airflow became controlled by levers. The original analogue clock was deleted at this point, as was that traditional surrounding ring to control the level of fan-assistance.

The unique interior feature for the 1976 Six was the development of an 8-light check-control unit that monitored functions from oil level to brake pad thickness and rear light operation. All without the need to leave the seat. Other advanced 6 Series electronic information systems (debuting a year in advance of the 7 Series) included an optional on-board computer and the Service Interval Indicator.

These race and crowd-
ed pit-stop pictures of
the Quester 635 bring
us closer to the atmos-
phere of Europe's sec-
ond-best-known 24-
hour race: the Spa 24-
hours in Belgium.
The start shot recalls
how hard it was to win
races in 1986 with
strong opposition to
conquer from Rover
(alongside the quickest
BMW), Volvo, and
Ford. The Bimmers
were usually out-quali-
fied, but won regularly
in longer European
events (including this
one) and made their
winning mark in
Australia and New
Zealand.

Pictures: Courtesy BMW
Archiv, 1998

There was no tailor-made series for the 635 to race in the States, but individuals still had fun with the big Bimmer coupe long after output had ceased. Here, an M6 owner soaks up the Sebring atmosphere on a BMW CCA Oktoberfest driving day.

Picture: Author, Florida, 1992

How the 02 was honored in the 1990s. This two-door blend of coupe style and sedan practicality was the definitive turning point for BMW's US credibility and commercial success. The 2002 is seen here in the 1990s, gathered in a line of round taillights at Laguna Seca Raceway.

Picture: Author Monterey, 1996

The way they were. The 503 made elegant use of the postwar aluminum BMW V8 and re-established BMW's credentials as a provider of classy coupes. The styling was by New York-based designer Albrecht Graf von Goertz. Less than 420 were made around the 140-bhp power train from its 1955 show debut to the close of the 1950s.

Picture: Author
Brochure of 1955–56

BMW 503 – das sportlich-elegante Cabriolet und Coupé

The 700 was an important for BMW, while the CS (Coupe Sport) cousin was a tiny ancestor to the six. This is the two-door coupe, which was offered with 30 to 42 horsepower in various developments between 1959–65, but BMW also created an astonishing 188,121 sedans.

The rear-engined mini-Porsche is often overlooked, but its twin-cylinders and agile handling proved particularly effective in rallying and racing, posting results way beyond its sub-1-liter capacity. This important US survivor appears courtesy of the Vasek Polak collection.

Picture: Author
Monterey, 1996

1990s tribute to a 1930s BMW classic on a 1960s BMW icon. Arthur Porter's 1800 "Tisa" racer carries this beautiful homage to the racing 328 on its pristine flanks. It was created by artist Dennis Simon, who also did great poster work for the 20th Anniversary of Motorsport Oktoberfest gathering held in Florida in 1992.

Picture: Author Monterey, 1996

Sporting silhouette. BMW's first truly sporting two-seater was the 315/1, and it showed the British Frazer-Nash establishment how to win team prizes in the 1.5-liter classes of early Alpine rallies. Deploying a redeveloped triple carburetor version of the in-line six-cylinder engine, it offered showroom customers 40 bhp at 4,300 rpm beneath those rakish lines. Owners—between 230 and 242 of them in the 1934–36 production span—expected up to 75 mph.

Picture: Andrew Yeardon MW GB, 1993

BMW history is fragmented, as this small selection from the L& C BMW dealer's collection in the UK demonstrates. From left to right: M1, UK specification (right-hand-drive) 328, Glas 1600 GT-BMW, BMW 2500 sedan, and one of the few authentic BMW CSL coupes in full "Batmobile" regalia.

Picture: Peter Osborne
Kent, UK, 1993

Knowing that the quickest coupe from BMW to wear the Stars and Stripes livery was this McLaren F1 GT-R, we show that BMW did find a way of winning the world's most prestigious sports car race with a showroom-related product. Propelled by a thoroughbred 48-valve V12 that developed over 600 bhp, a similar "Big Mac" won Le Mans upon its 1995 debut.

Picture: BMW AG
Le Mans, 1996

V8 and coupe cousins 503 (closest to camera) and 3200CS flank the 502 V8 sedan at Laguna Seca on the occasion of the BMW historic racing celebration weekend...sponsored by Chrysler!

Picture: Author
California, 1996

A pillar of the CS Register within BMW CCA in the US, Amy Lester's uprated 3.0 CS is always an eye-watering pleasure to photograph. The triple-Weber-carburated coupe had 270 bhp when I saw the car at a 1990s Oktoberfest meet.

Picture: Author
Sebring, 1992

This unique US coupe collection features the four-cylinder 2000CS, the uprated CS, the 6-series, and the 850i. The biggest seller was the 6-series, at more than 86,000 units, versus 13,691 units for the oldest 2000C/CS line. There were 21,147 of the 3.0 CS derivatives (including CSi/CSL) manufactured out of a total of 44,237 type 2000C to 3.2-liter CSL variants. From 1989 to 1996, BMW constructed just 28,292 of all 850/840 types. With the exception of 1993, 8-series output plummeted after 1991.

Picture: Klaus Schnitzer
US, 1991

Here is the most beautiful 507 I have seen. It wore Philadelphia dealer plates in 1996 and was the darkest blue this side of black. As for the 503, the 507's style was created by Albrecht Graf von Goertz, but unlike the 503, it did not wear the traditional kidney grille. BMW figures released in 1992 point to production of 252 units in 1957–59.

Picture: Klaus Schnitzer Monterey, 1996.

Wet or dry, on tarmac or pushing into the lush green lawns of England, the 6-series provided entertaining handling.

Picture: David Shepherd, 1998, Courtesy BMW Car magazine

The (in)famous electronic check board debuted on the 6 Series and lasted until 1989. It did not prove a "must-have" item like the Service Interval Indicator, which spread throughout the BMW range.

The original functions it monitors (as given in the small German type) are: 1, test activate elongated button; 2, cooling water level; 3, motor oil level; 4, brake fluid level; 5, brake lights; 6, rear lights; 7, windshield (and headlight option) washer fluid level; 8, brake-pad wear warning light.

Drawing: BMW AG, 1976
BMW Archiv 1998

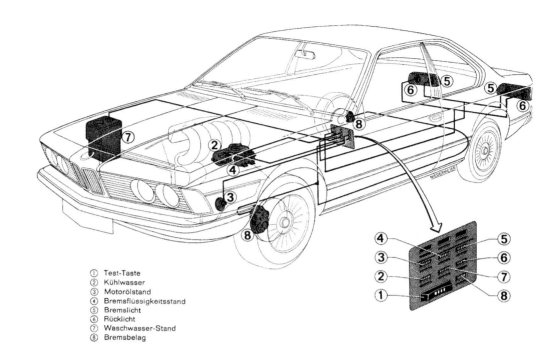

1 Test-Taste
2 Kühlwasser
3 Motorölstand
4 Bremsflüssigkeitsstand
5 Bremslicht
6 Rücklicht
7 Waschwasser-Stand
8 Bremsbelag

More detail on those features as we cover the launch models, but with that wonderful author's gift of hindsight, we can see that the 6 Series was as important for the electronics it premiered as for its bold and apparently timeless lines.

Only the multiple light check system (referred to by BMW with prophetic marketing skill as an "Active" panel) has not made it in its original format to the nineties. Service Interval Indicators are to be found right down to 3 Series Compact today, while the computer theme has been expanded considerably to overcome the original criticisms of complexity and poor positioning for viewing safely when mobile.

Generally, BMW computer readouts of average speed, fuel consumption and temperatures have tended to stay on the options list for smaller BMWs. The Service Interval Indicator has become standard equipment, red-lighting owners and nagging at the need for regular maintenance.

At the heart of the BMW cabin features was that clear instrumentation, distinguished at night by a dull orange glow, softly reminiscent of an airplane cockpit. BMW did not invent the clarity of single clear pane viewing, but they had always provided clear instrumentation.

Left- and right-hand-drive steer story: either way, the interior of the BMW 6 Series remains a beautiful place to be. Here we can see the 8-button test board to the left of the original 4-spoke steering wheel (in left-hand-drive) with half cloth/leather seat trim and wooden gear lever knob for the manual shifter.

The British right-hand-drive coupe displays the optional leather in association with Recaro sports front seats, the later 3-spoke steering wheel, automatic transmission, and mildly facelifted instrumentation.

Pictures: BMW Werkfoto, 1976/Archiv, 1998 and David Shepherd 1998, courtesy *BMW Car* magazine

Unlike Mercedes, BMW disdained installation of oil pressure gauges and usually went for the simplicity of a larger speedometer and tachometer, these matched by smaller water temperature and fuel level gauges.

Instrumentation aside, the designers created a BMW interior that was inspired by the logical layout of the Five, presenting controls and information in easily identifiable clusters. I have heard few complaints, and the overall BMW impression was "I'm in command, Captain of the Bridge speaking," this despite the lower stance of a coupe. Graceful sweeps of the fascia brought controls within a handspan of the driver, and provided an accommodating yet efficient drive—especially when compared to the contemporary "you have to be kidding" gorilla stances the Italian motor industry demanded of their clientele from Ferrari to Fiat, via the more relevant (to BMW in Europe) Alfa Romeo.

Hindsight tells us that BMW should have provided vertical adjustment to complement the simple in-out telescoping of the original four spoke wheel in their luxury coupe. For shorter people (I am 5 ft 9 inches tall), the provision of a vertical height seat control lever is a bonus, one that answered the vertical steering column adjustment criticism in the minds of the BMW design team.

Detail development

A General Motors employee in the sixties, Walter Stork was charged with chassis development for BMW in the eighties. Herr Stork recalled that he "arrived at BMW in 1970. I was involved in many aspects of our engineering work, except for the engine." The detailing of the new coupe's mechanical layout progressed on the basis of what was available elsewhere within the BMW product line, rather than from an open engineering brief. "There was no plan for any 4-cylinder engines, so we knew the running gear would all have to work with a 6-cylinder range. One that had the objective of being easy, and fun, to drive. Our first engineering job was to assess what was available from the 5 Series, and what would be useful from the future, or older BMW 6-cylinder sedans. Remember, the 7 Series was not announced until 1977, so we were restricted in many cases to what had been engineered already for the 5 Series."

This was a key point, for the 6-cylinder, 2.5 liter 525 was not sold until a year after the 520/520i launch of 1972. The 528, utilizing the 2.8 liter inline 6 that would be part of the later 6 Series, was not available until 1975, by which time all major engineering on the 6 Series had been signed-off.

We discuss engines in detail as a separate item, but you need to know that the initial 6 Series offered only 3.0 and 3.3 liters.

Walter Stork recalled that an essential part of BMW's engineering approach for the coupe was "to avoid components of heavier weight. The Six was supposed to be lighter and more sporting. Please remember that the same parts in a 6 Series have an easier life than those parts in a 7 Series sedan, because of the curb weights involved. Taking out 100 Dm was not the point for a luxury coupe. We were not trying to save money, but saving 50 kg was important."

An excellent example of that weight-saving approach was in the use of a 5 Series based final drive and rear axles for the coupes, right up to the 635. "When they came along with the 24-valve engine for the Motorsport 635, then it was too much," said Herr Stork with a rare laugh. " Then we did have to change the rear gear set and casing, to that which has also been used on the 735. In turn that meant we must reshape the floor area around the differential for the M6/635."

Starting from the ground floor up, there was the same 103.3 inch (2626 mm) wheelbase to rework from the 5 Series floor pan in readiness for its role supporting the new coupe. Herr Stork explained, "In the floor pan, essentially we must change all the brackets for the attachment of new components, provide a new seating position, this to fit with appropriate steering to wheel angles for a lower and more rear-placed driving position."

Most important changes underneath were directed at ensuring 6-cylinder standards of braking and suspension could be attached to the 5 Series floor pan. That pan was at the 4-cylinder pre-production stage when 6 Series engineering began.

Although the dimensions of the 528's brakes in 1975 and the 630-thru 635 discs were identical, the 528 started its production life with solid discs, whereas the 6 Series had used 4-wheel ventilated discs in most models from its inception. The dimensions shared by 528 and 630-633-635 were 11 in (280 mm) front discs and 10.7 in (272 mm) rears.

The 5 Series did get ventilated front discs eventually (1977), but retained solid rear discs for most of the life of the 6 Series. Thus the mountings for brakes and suspension on the 6 Series differed in detail, but BMW's sporting customers in racing, or at road car specialists Alpina, tend to treat the 5 and 6 Series very similarly during preparation.

For example, much of the 1982 Group A racing 528i technology, in itself sharing some components with the Group 2 racing CSL of past glory days, was transferred to the 1983 Group A racing version of the 635—one that BMW campaigned (and sold in kit form) from 1983 onward.

On the suspension side, Walter Stork kept the BMW tradition for classic rear-drive handling alive—a philosophy that has not been without controversy in a motoring world that accepts front-drive as the conventional, safe system.

Back then, BMW was made painfully aware that their Bavarian neighbors up at Ingolstadt had made competitive and commercial progress with 4 x 4 transmissions in the acclaimed Audi quattro format. In America, this quattro system did not make the commercial impact that one would have expected from a European viewpoint (Audi's "unintended acceleration" automatic transmission controversies hardly helped...).

In Europe, BMW was heavily criticized for not making sufficient technical progress at this time, especially in regard to aerodynamics and all-wheel drive. Today at least twenty percent of all Audis built have quattro 4x4 systems.

Back at the 6 Series pregnancy we found BMW's handling and road-holding principles were held as sacred. They extended throughout the early eighties front engine rear drive range—back then, BMW engineers shuddered at a mere mention of front drive.

Thus Herr Stork's thoughts on rear drive handling were of exceptional interest. "It is a conscious decision that we make, for 6 Series and the other cars in our range. It would be possible to make our cars without the power oversteer, but the price is that the car has a less exact feeling. So the car has less information feedback to the driver through the steering.

"We let the driver decide by giving him enough information, early enough to make up his mind. Drive fast on a curving road, and you will see what I mean. It is dangerous under these conditions to be in a car which is always understeering, always trying to make its way off the road with the nose first! There is no way to change its course.

"In our cars you can ease the throttle, or have some more speed; it's up to you. With a very powerful engine it is even more important to arrange things our way. It is not a philosophy that originated with me, but just what the customers want.

"For cars on dry roads, or at least not on ice, the BMW front engine, rear drive handling and roadholding is still a very good system. That applies for the foreseeable future, but for ice and conditions like that, yes, it must be four wheel drive (4-WD). At least it's a lot better than front drive! So you say OK to 4-WD, but then you ask yourself...How many people really want it? Then there is the extra cost, and sometimes the car does not feel so good.

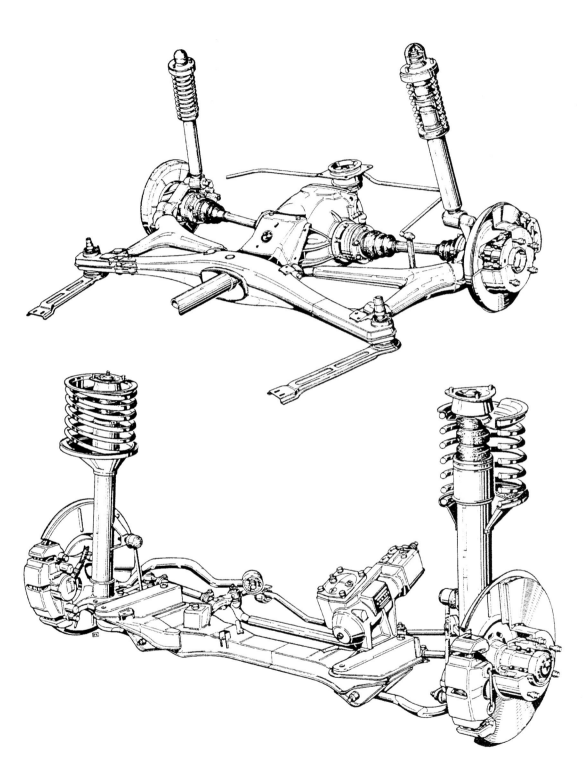

The front and rear suspension drawings reveal the 5 Series origins of the 6 Series, a model which had to wait upon either 5 or 7 Series engineering to progress its chassis. This is the redeveloped double-link front end with revised trailing arm angles at the rear.

In the nineties, the big owner preoccupation is to keep all the bushings tight, the solid-joint thrust links fresh, and the steering gear tight. Of all 6 Series major hardware, these items wear the fastest and can lead to repeated extra tracking and tire wear costs, nevermind the safety implications. Verdict: inspect steering and suspension components regularly!

Drawings: BMW
AG 1983

"In the 6 Series and the later developments that became possible, such as the 7 Series double link front suspension, or the new angle for the rear trailing arms that started in 528i, we could only go as fast as production would let us." Herr Stork reflected on a situation where the costlier 6 Series often had to wait for the high volume products to make a coupe engineering change economically possible.

There has been little complaint about the ride qualities of the 6 Series. There have been various layouts tried over the years, and there has always been the option of more sporting ride/handling compromise, available either through specially ordered parts as a kind of sport package, or through BMW Motorsport, or by simply trading up to the more overtly sporting choices such as 635CSi with the (initial) option of TRX wheels and tires that later became standard.

The later alternative was the M635, but it should be noted that the special Bilsteins and new springs supplied with this model actually provided a more absorbent ride than the TRX-shod standard 635CSi I took to Germany. Sportier does not always mean harsher!

On the ride subject Walter Stork recalled, "we did a lot of work to match the original 6 Series spring and shock absorbers to a natural frequency with the new seating. Some of this work was completed at Ismaning, some in disguised road prototypes, and we had our usual outings to the Nurbürgring as well.

"We also have some poor roads we use in Europe, but there are not many left, so I am not going to tell you where we did such work," said the BMW expert. In 1997 Britain it was found that a number of German engineers— including those of GM Europe—were coming to that island in search of the roughest roads in Europe; unfortunately they had tragic difficulties in adapting to the British habit of right-hand steering, and fatalities resulted.

Walter Stork resumed: "Generally we find a limitation to the gas-filled monotube shock absorber for our normal production models, so we regularly fit Boge or Fichtel and Sachs twin tube hydraulic dampers, which are able to differentiate between bump and rebound. For a sports option the gas-filled shock absorber is acceptable. If we use gas-filled shock absorbers, they are normally from Bilstein.

"In all cases we try to reduce the changes in track/camber and introduce more anti-dive. For the 6 Series this was only possible with higher mounting of the track control arm; the more power you have, the more anti-dive is required. The objective is always to provide the right dynamics. Not just away from the lights when the transfer of weight is a problem, but for all conditions.

"We try to give values the driver can always handle safely," concluded Walter Stork.

Engines Engineering

A quick dash to another BMW building in the suburbs of Munich—Fiz, the firm's vital central engineering HQ did not exist then—took us to the exciting spiritual heart of any BMW: engine research & development. Waiting nervously was a typically long-serving BMW employee, Georg Ederer. He was apprehensive over a lack of English practice, a contrast to the BMW marketing/PR people. As with all the BMW engine men it has been my fortune to interview, an overwhelming enthusiasm soon overcame the initial reserve. Information began spilling forth faster than I could legibly write it down.

I had to gauge the commitment BMW showed to engineering motor car engines, "not lorries as well," as BMW engineers ask you to remember in passing reference to the larger engineering resources of Mercedes. There were some 760 engine engineers at Munich on the passenger car program in 1983, and that was a sizable investment by any rival in the eighties.

Then, BMW Motorsport employed just over 100 staff and their responsibilities covered all the competition units for Grand Prix racing (M12/13 motors), as well as M12/7s for Formula 2 and sedans car racing, plus the detail development that went into M635, a subject we return to in chapter 7.

American readers may remember BMW in the turbo diesel car market, for there was an agreement with Ford US to supply the diesel six which BMW themselves used in European trim for the 524TD. Although there is a separate development department, along with the new plant at Steyr in Austria (a wholly BMW-owned subsidiary since April 1982, originally a co-development with Steyr-Daimler-Puch AG) BMW also did practical development work for Ford in Munich. Thus you could find larger American Fords sprawling all over the Motorsport department—or at the Ismaning test track—in the early eighties.

Back with our 760 engine men in Munich I discovered they had the use of 46 test cells "for functional use and another 22 for durability runs." Georg Ederer amplified, "such testing is at least twice as hard as when I first came here in 1966. Today we normally run at least 300 hours at full, full load which will probably be 6000 rpm or so, in the case of most 6 Series.

"That full load program must be five times what we used to do in the sixties. Then there are similar full load trials for things such as the differential to pass over 500 hours and the part load tests, where we run a mixed program for at least 1500 hours," explained Herr Ederer of the test work that endorsed BMW's reputation during the eighties.

Georg Ederer added, "Even then you cannot say this is all the test work behind a BMW engine, for there are millions, yes I really mean millions of kilometers to cover in cars. Winter testing in Sweden and Finland, plus other European locations. Hot weather testing? It used always to be North Africa, but now we do more, much more in the USA. In Africa the authorities were difficult and it is actually cheaper for us to test in America."

Such American road mileage research was also highly relevant to BMW as a large market, part of Georg Ederer's responsibilities covering emission and fuel consumption, all vital subjects in an American context for a European engineer.

Much of the department's time had been spent meeting American Emission standards. Part of the BMW manpower problem was that meeting US standards was not the same thing as complying with forthcoming European emission levels, or the differing standards imposed by then new markets such as Japan and Australia.

In the American market BMW had to supply different "Big Six" M30 derivatives, which we discussed with Herr Ederer first. All these sixes were SOHC chain drive descendants of the original 1968 "Big Six", rather than the M60-coded belt-driven overhead cam later design, which was installed in machines such as 320/520i, and 323i. The economical and slow-revving 2.7 liter Eta engine, was used in both the 3 and 5 Series of the eighties, but was dropped before that decade elapsed. The Eta engine used belt drive for its overhead camshaft and was developed from an M60 base, not the older 6 Series family of M30 motors.

Initial six cylinder coupe emission work concentrated on 6 Series' coupe predecessors. Between 1972 and 1974 BMW offered the 3.0 CS in American power trim. This had a low 8:1 compression ratio, the usual Solex carburetors, and was rated at 170 bhp SAE at 5800 rpm with 185 lb-ft of torque—roughly the same output as could be expected from the carbureted 2.8 liter engine in both coupe and early 528 for Europe.

As discussed, BMW dropped the old coupe for the American market because of roof legislation, but the 5 Series became relevant in the 6's life once more. Between 1975 and 1977 BMW offered the 3 liter engine within the acclaimed 530i. This mated 2985 cc with L-Jetronic fuel injection from Bosch. Herr Ederer recalled, "because we changed over

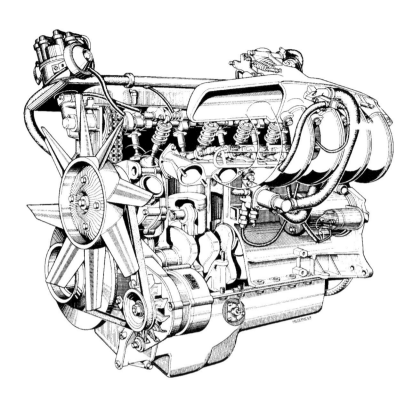

Constantly refined until the end of its production life at more than 670,800 copies in the early 1990s, BMW's M30-coded big sixes were at the heart of the 6 Series. The unit is capable of routinely absorbing mileages in excess of 150,000 with no major rebuilds required.

The double-roller, chain-operated single overhead camshaft (the assembly crowned by the distributor, top left) can need replacement in the 70,000- to 90,000-mile band if its oil feed becomes clogged, a common problem prompted by poor maintenance.

Drawing: Niedermeier, BMW AG, 1976, Archiv, 1998

from D-Jetronic for this purpose and also provided a thermal reactor, along with a low compression (8:1) and new engine ignition timing to make it pass the emission regulations. This engine was also used in the first American 630 model."

Thereby hangs a tale. For 176 bhp and 185 lb-ft of torque was not enough to offset the weight of 6 Series in Federal US form—some 3500 lbs leaving 0–60 mph times way adrift of what was expected in this price bracket, even though the BMW was usually tested by magazines in manual transmission trim against automatic gear box opposition.

BMW's injected six was looking for US friends amongst the critics, who usually plumped for Mercedes and Jaguar. This comment from *Car & Driver* in their December 1977 issue, comparing the $21,900 Jaguar XJ-S, $ 28,394 Mercedes 450SLC and $24,000 BMW 630CSi, was typical: "Third came the BMW 630CSi, far behind because of its lack of power."

So BMW went back to the tough task of providing a cleaner exhaust and seductive performance in a package that measured the best part of five inches longer than its European counterparts. BMW

The smallest motor in the European launch line was this 185-horse-power carbureted version of the M30 slant six, which was installed in the 630CS. Later, BMW had a better idea for Europe: the fuel-injected 2.8liter 628CSi, which ran until 1988. Just 1,651 units of the US Federal (fuel injection) 630CSi were registered in America for model years 1977–80, the bulk delivered in 1977 and 1978.

Picture: BMW Werkfoto 1976

won plaudits for the easy driving manners of the 3liter six, but a vehicle weight some 320 lbs plus over its European cousins was just too large an handicap to overcome.

Georg Ederer recalled the solution "a special version of the engine used originally in 733i and also in 533i, with a three-way catalyst for the USA." Again BMW marketing logic suffered a slight spasm, for this 89 x 86mm version of the fabled six cylinder engine measured 3210 cc and should have been badged 632CSi, but the badge budget was all used up at that stage!

Once more the 3210 cc motor used Bosch L-Jetronic fuel injection and the usual 30 degree slant installation, which did not harm the sweep of the 6 Series bonnet line at all. This power unit was to become the staple diet for big BMWs in the US and could be found in 5, 6 and 7 Series.

So far as 6 Series was concerned, the 633 model, European and American specification, was second only in sales popularity to the 635CSi. The factory shipped 23,432 , of which nearly 50 percent (11,939) were manufactured to Federal US specifications between January 1978 and September 1984.

An absolute godsend to BMW was the development of the Bosch Motronic engine management system with associated DME (Digital Motor Electronics). DME handled the enormous variety of loads placed on a production engine in a country like the USA, with its vastly varied climatic conditions and altitudes.

Looking over the American model years, power, torque and throttle response crept back into the specification as 3210 cc was adapted with its Lambda sensor and three way catalyst to cope with life across the Atlantic more efficiently. The original 8.4:1 compression of 1978 dipped to 8:1 and finally escalated to 8.8:1. That was close to the European level of 9:1 during the 1982–83 model years.

Similarly you could see power swarming back into the 3.2 liter Bavarian six, even for the US. In Europe, that 3210cc yielded 197 bhp at 5500 revs with some 200 lb-ft torque. For the US, BMW began in the 1978 season with 177 bhp at 5500 rpm and 196 lb-ft of torque at 4000 rpm.

When 1982 models went on sale, Robert Bosch's microprocessor electronics had helped provide American customers with 181 bhp at 6000 rpm and 195 lb-ft of torque at the usual 4000 rpm. The engine seemed happy to go for its 6400 rpm redline and provided *Car & Driver* with 124 mph and an EPA-estimated 19 mpg. Furthermore, acceleration times of 7.7 seconds and 16 seconds respectively for the 0–60 mph and standing quarter mile sprints were quoted.

That was in June 1983 and the price tag reported by C&D for the 633 CSi was $39,210. Gulp. That was nearly double the figure American journalists had been complaining of for the original 630CSi...

European Engines

Georg Ederer also conscientiously guided us through the development sequence for Europe, where the big pre-production change was a last minute abandonment of a 625. A 2.5 liter version of the previous coupe was made between 1974 and 1975 as a direct result of the fuel crisis and to show that BMW was not speed crazed by CSLs and the ill-fated 2002 turbo street car; just 1044 were made.

Originally the 2.5 liter's 150 bhp and 156 lb-ft of torque was scheduled for 6 Series, but even in the previous pillarless coupe the weight had been 3080 lbs (1400 kg). The idea of that 2.5 liters powering an ostensibly sporting coupe, one that weighted at least 100 lbs more than its predecessor, was finally enough to axe the project.

Coded E24 within the factory (E9 was the designation for the previous coupe; E simply stands for *Entwicklung*: German for development), the 6 Series for Europe came in two initial engine sizes. They possessed either a bore and stroke of 89 x 80mm for 2985 cc with quadruple choke Solex carburetor, or 89.25 x 84mm for 3210 cc with the L-Jetronic fuel injection.

The carburetor-fed 3liter was a little more powerful, with 185 bhp at 5800 rpm, than it had been in the 3.0CS (180 at 6000 rpm). Maximum torque was unchanged, but developed 200 rpm lower.

Why? Instead of CS-specification twin Zenith 35/40 INAT downdraft carburetors, BMW had selected the single Solex 4A1 design. In Ederer's opinion, "this Solex design was from American V8s and was usually called Quadrajet. It was an excellent carburetor and was a big advantage in progressive power over the twin Zeniths. The Solex was also easy to adjust and delivered an excellently controlled fuel/air mixture—but to service and manufacture this carburetor was a big problem for us," the forthright BMW engineer admitted.

Ederer advised us, "over the years we did much work on good mixture distribution with these carburetors. Always you seem to get liquid fuel delivered for some cylinders! So I am glad carburetors have gone on the BMW six cylinders. Now it is all taken care of automatically.

"Bosch receive test and development engines and cars from us and do much development work of their own. We also meet twice a week on average, and we always have a large number of Bosch engineers working here at BMW as well.

"We were not the first to fit electronic injection from Bosch, but they had the idea for us to try the Motronic system first. I think it is because they were used to working with us and the department was small enough and dynamic enough to work with this new system. Fortunately it gave us no problems at all in service. In fact it gets rid of many service troubles," was Georg Ederer's cheerful summary.

It was July 1979 before BMW engineers were able to reveal this electronically enhanced step forward, with its 256-point mapping memory, all initially available for the L-Jetronic equipped 3210 cc motor of the 732i and 633CSi, which we detail later.

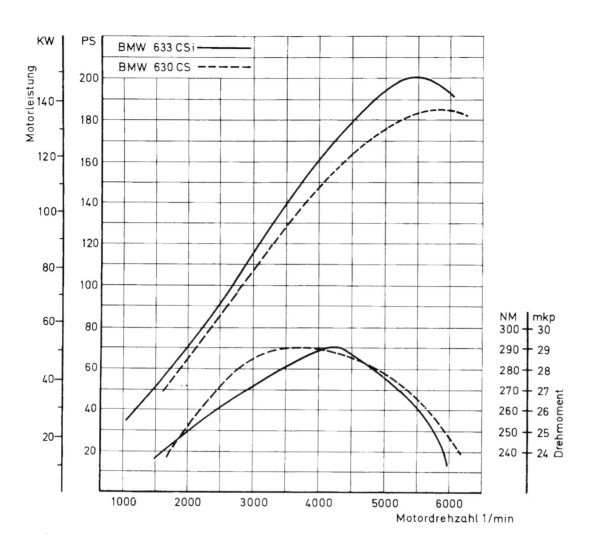

Contrasting power
curves are for the
debut 630CS (carbu-
reted 3liter) and 633CSi
(fuel-injected 3.3liter)
in European specifica-
tion. There was 15
horsepower between
these slant sixes, but
retaining fuel injection
at peak efficiency and
paying for its fuel con-
sumption ensured that
the carburetor's days
were numbered in this
BMW flagship: all
American models were
fuel-injected.

Drawing: BMW AG 1976
BMW Archiv
reprinted 1998

Meanwhile, there was another 6 Series that did not make the February 1976 pre-production plan. Why was there no turbo 6 Series counterpart to the 745i?

The good Georg Ederer shuffled his papers a little restlessly at this question of a power source that some American customers retrospectively fitted from Korman or Callaway. After much thought he replied, "certainly this turbo was considered and we examined the coupe carefully with this possibility in mind.

"We did some paperwork in the seventies on this subject, but the big question was where to put the intercooler? There simply was not the same space in the engine bay that you can find in the 7 Series. This would have been very expensive to solve, and we did not carry on with the project," he explained with a pensive grin.

Since the 635 was an add-on to the original program, we could see BMW had been serious about producing a less overtly sporting coupe for the eighties. I then gathered from our engineering visit, and other 1983–4 sources, that a 745i coupe equivalent was a much later consideration, for the 256 bhp version of the faithful 3210 cc did not appear in the saloon until July 1979 . Alpina did provide a turbo charged 6 Series that delivered 330 bhp under the B7S badge.

Now, the body beautiful that BMW wrapped around proven components.

QUICK FACTS

Models

630CS/633CSi, European and Federal US

Period

1976–1984

Production

Total 5766 of all 630CS (1794 to US specification)
Total 23,432 of 633CSi (11,939 to US specification)

Performance

In the US, 630CSi recorded 0–60 mph in some 10 seconds and reached 122 mph. European 633CSi recorded 0–60 mph in 8 seconds, averaged 133 mph maximum

People

Designer Bernhard Osswald, Karlheinz Radermacher (board member responsible for engineering development)

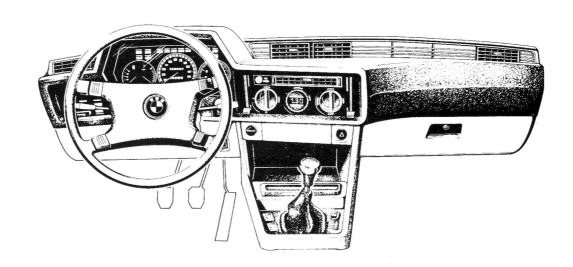

5 "A Legitimate Successor"

The key words above were spoken at the introduction of the new large BMW coupe 630CS/633CSi in Spain and highlighted the problem of following such illustrious predecessors...

March 1976: BMW was ready to publicize their new E24-coded coupe thinking in Marbella, Spain. The round of European Motor shows, particularly the annual springtime ritual of Geneva, was just around the corner, so it was time to spread the "Good Word."

Bernhard Osswald had retired when the public announcement of the 6 Series was made, his successor, Dr. Karlheinz Radermacher taking over as "member of the managing board of the Bayerische Motoren Werke AG for development."

Herr Osswald was on hand to answer questions and Radermacher—who would be responsible for top level BMW engineering decisions until his abrupt 1983 departure in the wake of controversy over 3 Series quality—paid positive tribute to Bernard Osswald's development team work. Dr. Radermacher said, "I wish to point out that it was my predecessor under whose direction this car was conceived, developed and perfected."

Dr. Radermacher went on to include the following remarks in an eight-page presentation. "The lot of a successor is not an easy one, especially when the predecessor was a particularly successful type....So, in developing the new coupe our sights had to be set correspondingly high. It had to be a legitimate successor."

As when the 3 Series replaced the sporty 02 two door, BMW was rightly concerned that some sectors of the press and public would not take to the more civilized, heavier comforts of the newcomers as compared to the legendary sporting success of its predecessors.

Judging from the heading "Munich Masterpiece" in the May 1976 *Motor Sport* over an introductory story by Clive Richardson of generally warm tone, BMW need not have worried. With hindsight it is possible to see that the company may have underestimated the sporting aspirations of their customers, typified by the 1978 debut of the 635CSi and the 1983 M-power derivative that emphasized this pattern to pursue more power at higher cost.

To put the BMW launch into the perspective of the times, the fuel crisis was a fading two year old memory, with BMW making particularly good forward financial progress. The 1976, BMW four wheelers ranged from the 75 bhp 1502, the last vestige of the 02 line hanging on in the wake of economy conscious motoring, to the 3.3L, long wheelbase version of BMW's biggest pre-7 Series sedan.

Between the 02 and those now aging large sedans, the BMW range made simpler sense with earlier versions of the models that we have today. For example, the E21 variant of 3 Series ran from the four cylinder 316 with 90 bhp to the 320i with 125 horsepower. All had two doors, prior to the 1982 E30, which debuted four-door motoring in the 3 Series.

Next up in 1976 was the 5 Series, which ranged from a 90 bhp 1.8 liter four cylinder unit to a carbureted six cylinder 528 with 165 bhp. The largest sedan range comprised, until the 1977 introduction of the 7 Series, BMW's 2500, 3.0S and 3.0Si with L for *Lang* (long) derivatives, which had an extra 3.9 inches in the wheelbase and a choice of 2.8, 3.0 or 3.3 liter fuel injected sixes.

Factory figures show manufacture of the 633CSi from September 1976 and the first Federal 633CSi models in January 1978—the latter fully two years after European output of the 633 commenced. Looking at the factory 630 output, one can see that they had two primary problems in the US: making the motors that met the emissions regulations of the 49 states and the 1978 California catalytic converter specs, and the performance of the 633CSi.

Despite the fact that it was a potentially more efficient fuel-injected version of the six in the USA, while carburetor induction was retained for European 630s, the US version was less powerful (176 versus 184 bhp). The US 6 Series also had to haul more than 300 lb/150 kg of Federal flab.

Unsurprisingly, this technically-induced reluctance to perform came across to the customers and the auto magazine road testers. The 0 to 60 mph run of approximately 9.5 seconds from the automatic version, coupled with a top speed shy of 125 mph was not impressive by previous 3-liter BMW coupe standards. There simply was not enough of an incentive to trade older coupes into 6 Series, or from a rival Mercedes or Jaguar over to a BMW successor that had also taken too long to get stateside.

"A symbiosis of functionality, aesthetic styling and outstanding performance," were the heady words used by BMW's press department to describe the most exclusive two-door in the BMW range. Note that the German market still allowed a single door mirror in the late seventies and early eighties.

Picture: BMW Werkfoto, 1982

So 633CSi sales were slow, under 1,400 for its sole 1977 model year on the US market at an initial $23,600 base on the East Coast and $23,700 delivered in the West.

Thus the 633CSi was the primary model available in the US from the 1978 model year to 1984, almost 12,000 were made to US specifications. The late 1984 advent of a Federal 635 finally nailed the performance objections of the US market and—as for Europeans—it was the most popular 6 Series, although the margin was tighter with some 13,000 made to varying Federal specifications—full details in our appendices.

The 633CSi was initially priced positively under $30,000 ($25, 495 East Coast) but by 1980 it listed at $29,465, with more luxury items incorporated, and had reached $35,910 in 1982. The 635CSi in Federal trim took the price process still further, pushing beyond $41,000 when tested by the independent major magazines in 1985. The compensation was the first US 6 Series capable of exceeding 130 mph and 0–60 mph in the low eight second bracket, provided you specified manual transmission and the $390 limited slip differential option.

British 6 Series customers waited far less than the US market. In October 1976 the UK received the right-hand drive (RHD) 6 Series, but the UK took only the 633 CSi injection model for the first two years. The carbureted 630CS was never officially imported to either Britain or America. In UK terms, the contemporary BMW range then began with the £3118 old 2-door 1502, the 3 Series starting at £3849 in 1976, while the 633 Csi quadrupled that, priced from £14,799 in Autumn 1976.

Original specification: Europe & USA

At the heart of any decision to buy a coupe rather than a sedan must be an appreciation of the styling. Paul Bracq and the small BMW team had completed a body that drew admiration even from engineers within BMW, a body of men more impressed by effective performance than refined elegance.

One senior engineer told me that obtaining all round visibility, while complying with the tough crash testing procedure with extra thick roof pillars, had proved the major development headache of the body. Design time spent juggling the driving position inside the cabin proved worthwhile and front seat occupants were usually well-pleased with the space offered, but those under 5 ft 6 in will find the hood a distant—and largely unseen—mystery.

The European weight penalty compared with the previous CSi line did not seem punitive. Considering the extra sheet metal had been crash test proven, the engineering figures seemed reasonable, until you made a comparison such as the European 3.0CSi versus the early American 630CSi. A little light math revealed a 480 lb weight gain for the US car, which had 14 bhp less to deploy. No wonder early US customers were unhappy, especially as the replacement coupe took so long to cross the Atlantic...

The European engineering argument from Munich compared the 6 Series (E24) with the previous E9-coded coupes. BMW engineering cited 1450 kg for the 630CS and 1470 kg for 633CSi compared to 1400 kg for the carbureted E9 and 1420 for the injected 3-liter 3.0 CSi predecessor to the 633 CSi.

However, even in Europe, you could see BMW Motorsport's reluctance to adopt the 6 Series as a racer was based on colder facts. The Munich factory had listed the CSL's weight at 2563 lb (1165 kg) (rather

The European launch of the 630CS and 633CSi range of 1976 landed in America as the 630CSi of 1977, while the 633CSi arrived one model year later. The lines were handsome, but aerodynamic efficiency was not the priority it became in the 1980s.

Picture: BMW Werkfoto, 1976

than the heavier public figures quoted in the previous chapter), providing a first class basis for sport that never had a 6 Series equivalent. That meant the previous generation six cylinder coupes could be built around 1000 lbs lighter than the first Federal 6 Series! Road legality would not have been possible in the US, but what a blast of a car that was with license plates attached!

Back in 1983, BMW engineering also highlighted weights for the rival Mercedes 280/350/450SLC coupes (1550 to 1630 kg) and for the Porsche 911 designs of the period (from 1120 to 1195 kg) which even then included the Turbo, a 260 horsepower/150 mph 3-liter.

Talking to Bernd Quinzler, responsible for international BMW advertising in 1984, I found that BMW strategy had been to pitch product as a halfway house between Porsche sportiness and Mercedes quality/civilization. Naturally it was BMW's contention that their customers would receive the best of both worlds in the new 6 Series package.

Although it was built on a common 103.3 inch (2626 mm) 5 Series wheelbase, the 6 Series used considerable front and rear overhangs to build prestige, and overall length, to a strong suggestion of 7 Series size.

Thus it measured 187.2 inches (4755 mm) compared with 181.9 inches (4620 mm) for the 5 Series and 191.3 inches (4860 mm) for the 110 inch (2795 mm) wheelbase 7 Series. The width was closer to the 5 at 67.9 inches (1725 mm) for the new coupe (less than an inch more, some 25 mm, than for 5 Series) with a fashionable low look supported by a roofline measurement of 53.7 inches (1365 mm) for the first 6 Series. Some 55.7 inches (1415 mm) was the comparable statistic for the boxy four door sedans in 5 Series. A 7-Series saloon was taller still, so BMW stylists had successfully produced a lowline coupe cousin with strong family identity and logic.

Today there is a lot more concern over aerodynamic efficiency than in 1976. BMW did not have their own wind tunnel until the eighties, and it showed in some of the independent wind tunnel tests performed on the range a decade later, with figures well above 0.40, the company norm until the eighties facelifts. Indeed some models in the BMW range rated at over 0.45 Cd before 3 Series was facelifted in 1982.

At the time BMW said, "tests conducted in wind tunnels have shown that the bodywork of the BMW 630CS makes this car the most aerodynamic of all standard BMW models produced until today. The small front spoiler underneath the bumper has quite a considerable influence on this good aerodynamic behavior, and thus on the outstanding directional stability, resistance to wind from the side, roadholding and economy of the

Badging and cockpit detailing are revealed. The analog clock was replaced by a red digital LED device in the shipments that reached the US during 1981.

Picture: BMW Werkfoto, 1976

new coupe. In fact, the new coupe is 21 percent better than the BMW 3.0 CSi in counteracting the upward pull of winds from beneath the car." Note that BMW would not make the comparison with the CSL, especially in winged format.

There were changes that improved both downforce and Cd figures for 6 Series, especially the advent of front and rear spoilers for the 635 (initially only the front air dam was standard in the US). The first editions of 6 Series specification laid the body story on a foundation of crash safety, all round visibility and cockpit layout with styling reference back to that 1972 Turbo design study as a source of inspiration.

Compared with the pillarless predecessor, 6 Series exhibited a quoted 69 percent extra torsional (twisting) strength and an extra 23 percent bonus in sheet metal "crush zone". You might have cursed the extra weight in the name of performance, but when an immovable object filled the windscreen at inevitable crash speed, crush zones suddenly became welcome and relevant...

Cabin comfort was, and remains, exceptional. BMW's headline story was the test-branded array of seven green lights that hopefully illuminated on depression of the test button. "Hopefully," because that indicated that all was well with engine oil level, brake fluid, brake lights, cooling water level, windshield washer level, taillights and brake pad thickness.

This test board idea has since been widely used in the BMW range, usually working without the driver having to press a button, but did not catch on totally in its original format. The basic principles were also be found in many of the fashionable digital dashboards from other manufacturers during the eighties.

In the original 630CS/633CSi you can see the shape that ran through the eighties with little modification. There was deliberate creation of the wrap-around cockpit feel to the cabin. In the LHD for 1976, you would grasp a sturdy four spoke steering wheel amidst an interior notable for the wide use of BMW-developed and manufactured plastics.

The horn buttons were inlaid into each steering wheel spoke. Ahead, under that single viewing pane, were three large dials: combined fuel-water-temperature gauges, a 140 mph (240 km/h) speedometer (with separate total and trip odometers), plus a 7000 rpm tachometer that was red-lined from 6500 onward.

Steering column levers controlled the traditional quick-action functions such as flashing indicators, headlamp flasher and windshield washers. The central fascia sweep carried some switchgear—notably the small

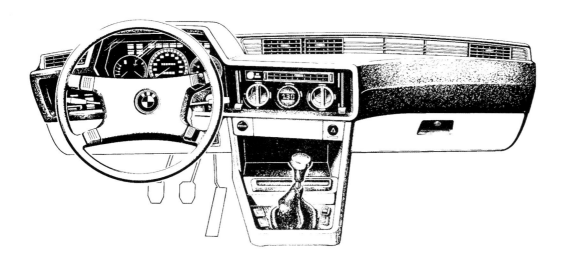

The 1980 model year European cabin shows the digital center clock in place, but the instrumentation and steering wheel remained as at launch.

Drawing: BMW Press, 1980

push-button that illuminated when the rear window elements were activated, and the heater/ventilation controls. These included the variable fan speed control, capable of fooling any stranger, being operated via the clock's bezel ring.

Electric windows, where fitted, were commanded from switches either side of the gear lever and activated all four windows, the rears notably slow in their limited action.

Initially there was a four speed manual transmission, the Getrag 262/9 with Borg Warner synchromesh components, or the three ratio ZF HP-22 automatic transmission with Fichtel and Sachs torque converter. Both 630/633 shared these gearboxes and a 3.45 final drive ratio was standard for 630CS, with 3.25 for 633CSi.

In general, BMW transmissions were a complex subject, more particularly the availability of myriad options. An author was unwise to be inflexible stating that a particular year must have a particular specification. For example, it was hoped that all UK 6 Series CSi models would come with a limited slip differential set at 25 percent locking as standard, and the publicity material reflected such hopes. That did not happen for these initial coupes, but Britons may well find a coupe in which the owner did specify an optional LSD.

As for a five speed gearbox in later cars—which could have closer sports ratios or the overdrive fifth and wider intermediates—the 6 Series owner learns transmission versatility. This applies even to the operation of later automatic gearboxes, for the ZF four speed of the eighties also allowed Sport or Economy modes, plus an individual gear lock-up—never mind what you could find on the central stick selector. Electronics are a mixed blessing at BMW...

In America, the 1982 model year 633 CSi was specified with a five speed gearbox as standard, the fifth gear added to the previous four speed ratios. Numerically raised final drive numbers would be used to offset performance losses and restore acceleration; for example, the US 635 used a 3.45:1 rear end ratio whereas the Euro spec 635 had a 3.07 rear end, manual or automatic transmission.

The 1976 Euro 630/633 models had four speeds with the following gear ratios: first, 3.85 ; second, 2.203 ; third, 1.402; fourth, direct 1:1. These were exactly as for the previous coupes, which also used the 3.25 or 3.45 final drives for the launch range in Europe.

The ZF automatic offered planetary gear variations based on: first, 2.478; second, 1.478 and a 1:1 third and final ratio. All the manual models used a single, hydraulically operated, dry plate clutch (MF 240).

Compared with the previous pillarless coupes, the new BMW's body advantages were not confined to the extra strength of the integral roll-over hoop within the center B-post pillar. Luggage capacity was up by 23 percent to 14.6 cubic feet instead of 11.8 cubic feet. In practice this meant two British journalists could buy crates of duty-free French booze, add it to the personal debris and luggage accumulated in a week's travel across three European countries, and still close the trunk without rupturing the hinges.

The accent on creature comforts, compared with earlier BMW two door coupes, was apparent in the use of 91 lbs of sound insulating material, instead of 50 lbs. Similarly the glass area was up, somewhat surprising in view of the need for extra pillars on 6 Series. BMW said the increase was 7 percent. A bit more important to those in sunny climes was that Parsol Bronze heat resistant glass was standard, whereas it had been a special equipment item on the 1968–75 coupes for Europe.

Seating was sharply improved over previous standards and included provision for driver's seat ride height adjustment in the basic 6 Series specification. Confirming the emphasis on comfort, heater output was boosted from 6500 kcal to 8000, up 23 percent. More important, the previous BMW weakness in flowing air through a cabin with extensive glass area (coupe and 02 Series) was plugged with plenty of adjustable fascia outlets and a 31 percent increase in cabin air flow. For the US in particular the air conditioning was asked to provide 6200 kcal refrigerating capacity over the earlier 4500 kcal CSi designs. The alternator remained rated at the 770 watts of late model 3.0CS/CSi coupes, but battery capacity went from 55 amp/hr to 66.

Engine moves

Underlining the work put in by Georg Ederer and his colleagues, detailed in the previous chapter's interview, was a long list of specific changes made to the installed inline sixes for the new coupe.

The carbureted 630CS and the injected 633CSi were notable by today's standards in selecting a common 9:1cr instead of the 9.5:1 that had been available in the European 3.0CSi. Eighties coupes reverted to the trend for increasing, rather than reducing, compression ratios in the quest for efficient combustion. By 1982 the European 635 was operating a 10:1 compression, while the American cousin stayed at 8:1 to meet Federal requirements.

Back in the seventies, European sixes used triple hemisphere combustion chambers within that 9:1cr layout in alloy, a design feature that promoted a swirling action within the combustion chambers. Such principles were basic to BMW's belief in maintaining a good proportion of European power in countries with stricter emission laws, and initially allowed BMW life on the American market with less emission control equipment than most rivals.

How fuel was delivered to serve in the combustion process showed continued seventies progress. Georg Ederer commented on the four choke Solex carburetion fitted to the 630CS in our interview and this was the reason for an extra 5bhp quoted 200 rpm lower than for 3.0CS of the earlier seventies, bringing the 1976 Euro coupe total to 185 bhp at 5800 rpm. The peak torque figure remained unaltered at 188lb.ft. but here the newer coupe had to go to 3500 rpm instead of 2700.

For the injected models, a Bosch L-Jetronic system meant the more sensitive detection of airflow rates within the fuel injection unit, via a meter to govern fuel proportions, while the previous D-Jetronic apparatus relied on partial vacuum measurement inside the intake manifold.

The 3210 cc engine in 633CSi thus developed the same 200 bhp at 5500 rpm as its earlier high compression 3-liter cousin, but the extra cubic capacity also brought 210 lb.ft. of torque at the power peak instead of 200 lb within 50 rpm of the previous figure. These 3.2 liter European figures were given at the launch; in 1984, the equivalent 3210 cc quotes were 197 bhp at 5500 revs and 209.5 lb.ft. at 4300 rpm, listed only for the 732i.

Engine cooling was given greater attention in the 6 Series with a Holset-coupled viscous fan of 16.5 in girth, up nearly an inch over previous six cylinder practice. A big change for the better around the SOHC six was the use of breakerless transistorized ignition for the 633CSi. The carbureted European 630CS stayed with coil and contact breaker systems and their attendant increased maintenance demands.

Steering a new course

New 6 Series owners who were familiar with examples of the 1968–75 BMW coupe range probably noticed a significant steering change at anything above parking lot speeds. The new design featured ZF ball and nut hydraulic power steering with a 14.5 steering box ratio (16.9 overall replaced the 18:1 overall ratio used between 1968 and 1975) but far more importantly the power assistance from the servo system was set to provide

The launch 630CS and 633CSi were civilized improvements over their predecessors, but quality problems enforced a clumsy build and assembly process at BMW soon after the press launch. In 1977, the bodies continued to be constructed at Karmann of Osnabruck, but assembly was shifted to the BMW Dingolfing plant, the facility that subsequently assembled all Sixes and Eights. This meant that the completed Karmann bodies endured a 373 mile railway trip to reach the BMW assembly plant.

Picture: BMW Werkfoto, 1976

less assistance at speed. This transformed the driver's feel of the power-assisted car, for as you went faster, the steering became heavier, just as tough as if it were a manual arrangement. Such power assistance is now commonplace, but only thanks to the efforts of BMW and Mercedes. The Germans ensured that the roads of Europe didn't have to be tackled in the traditional one-finger power steered manner popularized in American cars—or Jaguar's literally dead accurate rack and pinion layouts.

Steering input to a driver's palm was markedly different among those traditional rivals, Jaguar, BMW and Mercedes. The British car favored an extremely light action, made a little heavier with the deletion of one tooth from the rack, but still transatlantic in the minimal effort required at the rim. That the Jaguar rack and pinion is precision personified is in no doubt, but there is also a strong suspicion that drivers who buy machinery such as the 6 Series prefer to feel what is going on, particularly on the side of a frozen Alp! By the nineties Jaguar had seen the light and the XK8 combined informative steering rim effort with uncanny precision.

As implied by our eighties interview with Walter Stork, a great deal of general chassis work was devoted to making the 6 Series a far better choice than one might have expected from the retention of the usual MacPherson strut front and trailing arm back end that is the BMW tradition.

Before becoming too warm about how much better the Six was than its predecessors, it is relevant to note that the old coupes were nothing special in the handling department. Good fun, but not particularly efficient at restraining the inevitable waywardness of 200 horsepower applied to a wet city street, one that had been lovingly finished in a slick of truck diesel to provide the kind of coefficient of friction skid schools adore.

The handling point was that the 1968–75 BMW coupes were continual updates of what had originally been a conversion from the early sixties BMW four doors with four cylinder power. The legacy was a narrow rear track: 55.2 inches (1402 mm) instead of the front's 56.9 inches (1446 mm). That fundamental point was tackled with a wider rear than front end on the 6 Series: 55.9 inches (1422 mm) leading 58.5 inches (1487 mm) at the back end.

Handling was fine tuned with reduced caster angles and increased kingpin inclination on all 6 Series, plus the use of a rear anti-roll bar that had not been generally available throughout the previous coupe range. At the front, anti-roll bar diameter increased to 24 mm rather than the old coupe's 23 mm, getting closer to a full one inch thickness, while the new rear bar was of a 0.63 inch (16 mm) diameter.

Camber angles were left the same at the front, very slightly positive: $0°\pm30$, a full degree more inclination than had been exhibited on the earlier coupe. At the rear, $1°30 \pm30$ was the specified camber angle. Again, this led to more chance of rear end grip under duress, but with negative camber angles the designer's problem is that a consistently heavily laden car will tend to wear the inside tire tread at a high rate, the inside doing more work under low cornering or heavy luggage loads with a negative camber layout. Negative camber is identified from the rear by the disposition of the wheel and tire, apparently splayed outward at the lower edge, often with the outside of the tire tread clear of the tarmac until the machine is actually cornering hard.

The comfortable character BMW had aimed at with the 6 Series was generally reflected by increased suspension travel figures, up to 4.5 inches at the rear end. The overall effect with the 633CSi was of a car less prone to follow bumpy road cambers than its coupe forbears. A 6 Series was appreciably more comfortable over bumps, but generally less sporting in character, although the speed-sensitive steering drew favorable comment world-wide.

Braking? As discussed, dimensionally the units had a lot in common with 5 Series, but were ventilated all round, rather than just at the front, as on the 528/528i. For BMW coupes, the major step forward was in uprating the old coupe's 10.7 inch (272 mm) ventilated discs into 11.0 inch (280 mm) fronts, retaining the same vented rear 10.7 inch layout. The caliper specification of the front discs remained the same through the size multiplication, but a pad wear safety warning was part of the 6 Series check system. The servo unit was a Mastervac 9 inch unit for 6 Series.

Note that a wide variety of options, particularly on the less extensively equipped German market machines, were offered right from the start. The January 1976-printed catalogue that I was given in Munich shows that an alert owner could have specified Recaro seating, three spoke sports steering wheel of 15 inch (380 mm) diameter, a 65 amp alternator, leather trim and a complete sports suspension pack, including the quaintly quoted "tilt angle stops on the front spring struts, modified front stabilizer bar, reinforced rear stabilizer bar, sports-tuned springs/shock absorbers."

As ever, there were a lot more extras, from air conditioning to headlamp washers, which were part of the basic specification in countries used to paying more for their BMWs, typically Britain. What you could get varied according to the market concerned.

For instance the standard wheel and tire combination was an alloy 6J x 14 H2 unit with 195/70 VR radials, frequently by Michelin for British examples. An American 633CSi started life with 7J BBS-Mahle alloy wheels, whereas the original US-market 630CSi offering had the usual alloys and visually different rear end bumper treatment.

The determined BMW enthusiast could find any number of specialists keen to fit individually tailored equipment, factory-made or otherwise. So you might well find an oddity such as a five speed gearbox or a 3.5 liter engine with front and rear spoilers among launch stock 6 Series, but BMW did not make it that way to begin life in the fast lane!

Performance

Although the whole launch philosophy was built around distinguished coupe heritage and style, rather than rampant performance, no 6 Series deserves to be labeled as anything other than rapid transportation for road use. There was not an immediate performance successor to the legendary CSL in the new BMW range, but what they had was enough to attract customers who Munich-based adman Bernd Quinzler described as being typically "above average intelligence. They may not see motorsport, but they are interested—and they have the personal qualities of a competitor, wanting to beat others. They do not like to show off: we have a slogan that we used that sums it up, 'Our status is not on the hood (meaning the marque badge - J.W.), it's underneath.' Our target group is one that likes understatement, and that is one of the reasons people call us conservative in our body styles....or worse!" Herr Quinzler concluded.

In the table you will find the km/h figures and UK/US equivalents provided by BMW at the European press launch for 6 Series performance. Independently timed performance figures for European and American 6 Series are to be found in Appendix 2.

(All times in seconds)

Speed	630CS	633CSi
0-31 mph (0-50 km/h)	2.7	2.6
0-50 mph (0-80 km/h)	5.9	5.6
62 mph (100 km/h)	8.9	7.9
0-75 mph (0-120 km/h)	12.4	11.4
0-99 mph (0-160 km/h)	23.4	20.9
1/4 mile (0-400 meters)	16.3	15.8
Maximum speed	130.4 mph	133.5 mph

In general these figures were realistic predictions of production performance, but American customers will remember that their 630CSi had a hard time breaking the 0–60 mph ten second barrier: the 1978 model year 633CSi in Federal trim was 5.5 seconds slower from 0–100 mph than its European counterpart. Top speeds would have been around 122 and 125 mph respectively for those two US-bound coupes.

Fuel consumption?

In the US, around 18 mpg was the commonly averaged figure for independent testers. BMW NA—just as for the UK BMW importers—usually hit their journalists with more efficient manual transmission models that were unlikely choices in the US market within the luxury category.

When it was found that the later automatic European 635 would give improved mpg and excellent performance figures, then that was released freely to UK journalists, and it was just such a model that I took to Germany to conduct the original research for this book, and which I now own.

Hitching up an automatic to the earlier sixes in 6 and 7 Series did hurt imperial mpg badly in British conditions. One of the major BMW dealers reported, "London users can get down to a regular 14-15 mpg with an early auto and 17 mpg is not uncommon out in the country. The newer (meaning early eighties) models are much much better." For a four speed manual 17-19 mpg seemed usual, these are figures for the fuel injected 633 CSi and likely to represent better overall consumption than 630 CS managed.

In action, the 633CSi in Federal 3.2-liter form was often out-gunned by its Mercedes V8 and Jaguar V12 opposition. However, sales exceeded 2,600 units a year in 1983–84, and only the 635 sold at a better rate.

Picture: BMW NA, 1982

Independent UK tests by *Autocar* and *Motor* in the UK generally showed better mpg than anticipated and at least the performance BMW predicted, if not more. *Motor* managed 134 mph maximum against *Autocar*'s 131 and *Motor* also held the 0–60 mph upper hand with 7.8 seconds reported against *Autocar*'s 8.1 seconds.

Both magazines returned closer to 21 mpg overall. In US terms those represent around 25.2 mpg and I can almost hear the hollow laughter across the Atlantic; the everyday probability for emission models was always beneath 20 US mpg in their original guise. The 1983 EPA Estimated figure for 633CSi was 19 mpg.

Did the customers take to the new coupes in 1976? Not without BMW making some swift changes....

QUICK FACTS

Production
1976–82

Models
Original 630CS, 633CSi to 628CSi
and first edition of Europe-only
635CSi

Performance
From 176 bhp Federal 630CSi to
European 218 bhp 635CSi

Evolution of the Sixer Species

Following the adored CS coupes was not easy and BMW had to make frequent quality and engine upgrades in production to meet American and European expectations of a new BMW flagship

Karmann at Osnabruck initially constructed the 6 Series just as they had been responsible for earlier BMW coupes, making seven pre-production 630s and ten 633s in 1975. When the car was publicly released the following year, Karmann manufactured 1154 of the 630CS in that first 1976 sales season. This followed the new BMW coupe's public debut in March at the Geneva show.

As ever in BMW coupe tradition, the more powerful and larger-engined variants tended to do better and Karmann made 2848 of the injected model in 1976.

If you look through 6 Series coupe production figures, the 635CSi was the only model to exceed 3400 units a year. So we are discussing a comparatively rare mass production model, as well as seeing that BMW's customers tend to go for the fastest and best-equipped derivatives in the coupe line, for the 635's best year (1985) saw it hit 7270 copies, about double the 3387 manufacturing peak for 633 during 1977.

However, all was not well at the start of the latest BMW coupe's career. The Americans were not overjoyed at the performance of their ex-530i fuel injection version of the 630 and BMW was seriously concerned with quality complaints that they felt rested with the coachbuilders.

Neither were press and public overawed by the performance of 630CS and 633CSi. There were the usual sharp comparisons with beloved BMW predecessors on the sporty side, for there was no CSL excitement allowed at this early stage in the new coupe's career.

BMW acted on the quality front to bring as much of the assembly job 'in-house' as fast as possible, also changing the American recipe with alacrity. From August 1977, Karmann were confined to making metal, delivering a steel bodyshell in primer by road to the sprawling and continually expanding buildings beneath huge chimneys at Dingolfing.

That arrangement continued into the eighties, using transport for a production rate that needed road transport flexibility. For deliveries had to match a demand that peaked in summer at possibly 55 coupes a day, and slumped to 30 or less in the winter seasons of 1983–4.

For BMW perspective you need to know that Dingolfing served to top up 3 Series production, making about 250 a day in addition to the 550 or so that they made in Munich in 1983.

On the same lines as the occasional 6 Series, Dingolfing's 14,100 workers averaged about 500 of the 5 Series saloons and about 200 of the range-leading Sevens. So the 6 Series coupes were a low production center of attention. However, it is only fair to say that, in May 1984, I and a colleague visiting Dingolfing were most impressed with the hard work and paint preparation/finish that went into *every* BMW. Today, I believe that E30-coded 3 Series of the mid-eighties were amongst the finest finished small sedans made by any company, anywhere.

Dingolfing employees, particularly those who fitted up sub-assemblies to the engine/gearbox/front suspension package offered up beneath each BMW, earned every Dm they got. For they kept precisely on the pace of a

How it was in the beginning. Karmann-manufactured 6 Series bodies arrive at the Dingolfing factory after their extended rail trip.

Picture: Author/Dingolfing, Bavaria, 1984

line that makes fewer cars than some European Ford Escort production plants—and did it with a finesse to satisfy a far more fickle public.

There were 800 quality control personnel to satisfy, 30 checkpoints to pass and a separate department that paid individual attention to coupes, with slightly different 1.5 hour road tests for every M635CSi/M6 imposed. All had a ten minute operational check on a rolling road.

Back in 1977, BMW was concerned that the trim fit and water leak problems were eliminated from the early 6 Series, and high pressure water tests continued to be part of the build and checking process in the mid-eighties.

In 1977, BMW also had to find some more power for the clientele and the Americans got priority (would I suggest they hollered loudest?) from the 1978 model year.

The answer was the Federal 633CSi based on the 3210 cc six cylinder engine that was shared for North American BMW use by the 7 and 5 Series, four door sedans. It had little more horsepower than the injected 3 liter that preceded it, but far better driving manners.

A useful torque bonus won the 633CSi a place in the market more worthy of the 1981 American catalogue description for 633CSi, "A high performance coupe, as opposed to a high performance facade." By then an 8.8:1 compression ratio had allowed 181 SAE horsepower and 195 lb-3ft of torque to restore some respectability to BMW's North American coupe performance. These 1978 model year 633CSi coupes also had the wide Mahle wheels and new rear bumper treatment to differentiate them from the original Federal 630CSi.

The most popular Sixer arrives

In Europe performance was a priority too. In July 1978 the Bavarian Motor Works presented the model which was to become the most numerically popular in production, accounting for more than half the 86,216 total output by 1989. BMW commented at the 635 launch, "introducing the 635CSi, BMW is launching the fastest four seat coupe made in Germany. A new model designated to supplement the 630CS and 633CSi series,"

In fact the 630CS stayed on for just another year. The 633CSi's sales task became America, and other lands, where its emission certified 3210cc six was vital. Markets such as Britain took the 633 as an automatic until 1980.

Looking good on the street and the sales graph. The 1978–89 performance and civilization package offered by the 635CSi proved to be the most popular of the 6 Series, accounting for more than half of total output. Some 45,213 were made, with just over 13,000 officially imported to the US and about 5,000 of those under the L6 badge.

Picture: BMW Werkfoto, 1978

The 635 did not get to the US until the mid-eighties (some seven years after it debuted in Europe) and was not the performance or sales performer for the US that it should have been. In fact, a Federal 635 had a job to pull a convincing margin over the US 633CSi, for the American 1983 model 633 CSi performance levels were pretty respectable.

Just 8.4 seconds were reported 0-60 mph on a test 633CSi, plus a 16.8 second standard quarter mile from *Road & Track* in 1982. This acceleration coupled to a two-way average of 124 mph in fourth rather than the overdriven fifth gear. Over $10,000 less and slightly quicker according to *Car & Driver* was the 127 mph (15.8 seconds over the standing quarter mile) BMW 533i four door. When the customer wanted a coupe, he had to want a coupe *really* badly!

As ever at BMW the essential excitement of the 635 newcomer lay in the engine. This 93.4 x 84 mm (3543 cc) SOHC six for 635 in 1978 Europe was credited to BMW Motorsport development. The cylinder block marked a rather daring oversize bore that Paul Rosche had originally been told was impossible when he had wanted extra capacity for the 'Batmobile' CSL coupes of 1973.

To emphasize that relationship, the 635CSi six was coded M90, acknowledging a cylinder block descended from the M49 racing engines of the seventies. Similarly, the M88-coded four valve per cylinder unit within the mid-engine M1 was also duly linked into M6, when that arrived.

Behind the fancy new
BBS Mahle "spider"
pattern alloys, the
European 635 offered
an 18-bhp bonus over
the regular 200-bhp
633CSi, as well as the
aura of a genuine
sports coupe.

Drawing: Niedermeier, BMW
AG, 1978/BMW Archiv, 1998

As introduced in the summer of 1978 there was no faulting BMW's
logic, for the 3.5 liter provided 218 bhp with 5200 rpm civility, plus a
torque curve that looked as though one could build a decent apartment
block on it. That broad spread of more than 191 lb-ft pulling power
between 2000 and 5900 rpm was the foundation for exceptionally solid
European performance, even with the automatic attached and the air conditioning on. The maximum torque report of 224 lb-ft at 4000 rpm was
almost incidental...

The 635 motor was the first of the 6 Series to follow the eighties bias
towards high compression ratios, rated at 9.3:1. Detail installation
changes that complimented the utilization of the bigger bore, shorter
stroke engine, included ensuring that the fuel/air metering of the Bosch L-
Jetronic fuel injection was updated. Exhaust gases could be more swiftly
removed too, for the exhaust pipe diameter went up from 633CSi's 1.65
inches (42 mm) to a sturdy nearly two inch bore (1.97 inches for pedants).

The MF 240 diaphragm spring clutch had its pressure plate springs
strengthened and a five speed Getrag 265/5.70 gearbox was standard equipment. The introductory ratios centered on a direct top and a raised 3.07:1
final drive in place of 633's rear end 3.25 and the earlier 3.45. A ZF limited
slip differential was frequently fitted, but remained clearly on the option list
in major markets. For example, in 1984 the UK was offered the limited slip
as standard on manual 635s and a £322 option with automatic.

Now with 140 mph pace and a conservative 0–62 mph acceleration
claim of 7.3 seconds (most independents got 7 seconds or less for 0–60
mph) Walter Stork's suspension men started specifying subtle suspension

modifications. Front spring travel remained the same, but at the rear the movement was stiffened and restricted, with heavy duty roll bars also specified front and back. "Anti-tilt blocks" to limit roll were also introduced to the front strut springs.

Most obvious chassis change was to the wheel equipment. 6.5 inch 'spider's web' BBS Mahle light alloy types replaced the usual 6 inch alloy. Tire size remained at 195/70 VR on the previous 14 inch diameter.

The 11 inch front discs and 10.7 inch rears were left alone, but a comprehensive glassfiber front spoiler in matching body color and a deformable plastic (later rubber) trunk lid air dam modified the aerodynamics while adding sales potential. BMW said they had reduced uplift by an average of 15 percent, which greatly improved directional stability at high speeds, although the firmer suspension added much of the increased driver feedback and confidence in the new coupe recipe from BMW.

Since the 635 did not arrive officially in America with the (marginally) bigger 3.5 liter unit, comment on that car in 3.4 liter trim appears in the following chapter. In its homeland, the 635 was seen as a unique niche player between Porsche 928 speed and Mercedes establishment sobriety. In the US that would be hard to understand, the Bimmer priced very highly for the performance delivered. In Europe, the combination of 140 mph pace and 7 second 0–60 mph ability was enough to earn it a valid place as a luxury performance coupe.

Britain got the 635CSi with RHD at a theoretical snippet under £16,500 and continued to receive the 633CSi, but only in CSiA three speed automatic specification at £15,379. I say "theoretical" in relation to 635's October 1978 launch cost, for a heavy armor plating of extra and supplementary charges was always a feature of RHD models. By June 1979, *Motor Sport* could report a basic cost of £17,199 and extras adding another £2132.

If you are buying second-hand in Europe, know that air conditioning originally cost over £1000 extra in the UK and a sunroof demanded more than £550, so fully-equipped cars represent better value overall. Note that from April 1980 RHD 635's had headlamp wash-wipe, heated door mirrors and passenger seat height/tilt mechanism as standard.

There was the gearbox option in Britain and mainland Europe of a direct top gear five speed, or the overdriven ratios (as specified as standard US equipment in the eighties catalogue I hold) as part of the standard specification; the close ratio sports gearbox alternative was a no cost option.

The 635CSi debut in Germany was announced in the national press campaign, linking its engine (actually, the cylinder block) with that of the fabled M1. At this time, BMW AG continued to offer the home market the 630CS, the 633CSi, and the newcomer.

Advertisement repro: BMW AG, 1978/1984

Der neue BMW 635 CSi.
Es gibt Ideen, die zu gut dafür sind, nur einmal eingesetzt zu werden.

By the later seventies, BMW had made some major 6 Series changes. These were announced for the German market in July 1979, and rode on the back of a heavily revised 7 Series. Major 6 Series addition was at the 628CSi start of the range, now all fuel-injected, as had all US models been since the start. Effectively the 628 base model replaced the carbureted 630C, which ceased production in July 1979 with just 5763 made, only 249 of them in that final production year

Not imported to the US was the European range entry point: 628CSi. The smoothest of smooth BMW inline sixes at 2.8 liters was familiar from the 528i. It was inserted with a European norm of 184 bhp. The usual sturdy dimensions of 86 x 80 mm (for 2788 cc) were equipped with the same 9.3:1 compression as the 635 had premiered. A 628 was reckoned to provide about 130 mph by the factory, and this claim proved realistic during independent tests.

The 628CSi weighed 154 lbs (70 kg) less than the original 635. As a result, 628 acceleration was still not far off that of the four door 528i sedan, which weighed over 200 lbs less. The 628 ran a claimed 9.0 seconds from rest to 60 mph (8.5 seconds for *Motor* in the UK), returned 25 Imperial mpg on 97 octane leaded fuel; the 628 was subsequently priced in the same UK bracket as Audi's five cylinder quattro turbo or the 3.6 liter Jaguar XJ-S six cylinder.

The 628 was not overburdened with standard equipment, looking almost obsolete without the usual spoiler "beard" of the 635 and many contemporary cars. For the British market it came with 6 x 14 inch alloys and Michelin 205/70 VR tires and lacked showroom-standard anti-lock braking, automatic transmission, air conditioning and a sunroof.

By contrast the 633CSi depended on the 7 Series 732i in Europe, both using the 3210 cc engine that had the Federal emission counterpart. It was rated at 197 hp at 5500 rpm and 210 lb-ft of torque at 4300 rpm in European guise. Both the 732 and 633 were also aligned with this summer '79 update in the use of a 9.3:1 compression.

This 3210 cc engine was also the first, and for a while the only European BMW six with the Digital Motor Electronics (DME) mated to the Bosch L-Jetronic injected engine. Engine ancillary changes included a new dual pipe exhaust unit with larger effective intermediate silencers and wide use of stainless steel.

The exhaust systems were also an imposing sight at the Dingolfing assembly plant, as can be the debit digits in your bank account, when the system eventually does come up for replacement at an official dealership. However, late nineties shifts in exchange rates were beginning to take the sting out of European BMW spares prices, particularly for older models.

Weight reduction was tackled in 6 and 7 Series by more efficient utilization of the sheet metal needed in safety crumple zones and non-load bearing areas in the unitary steel bodies. However, there was also a dietary aid in the form of an aluminum radiator which BMW claimed was "not only lighter, but also more efficient in cooling."

All BMW six cylinder engines used transistorized ignition without contact breakers, but microelectronics brought new possibilities to precise control of vital ignition and fuel feed functions. At the heart of the DME system was a mini-computer programmed to activate correct ignition timing, fuel and air mixture settings. The computer also set the precise moment to inject fuel under widely differing circumstances (from Alaskan cold start to Mojave desert workout) and accounted for varying barometric pressures and outside air temperatures in making such calculations.

Using an ignition performance graph with load and engine rpm mapping points, BMW reported "256 memory locations are obtained. Each of these memory locations can be filled with an individual ignition time. Due to the enormous speed of computation, at every revolution a new

Capable of almost 140 independently timed mph with acceleration to match, the 635CSi brought back performance respect to the BMW coupe line in Europe. The original body decals, including the spoiler definition lines on the lower front edges and many varieties of body-side stripes, is time-consuming today.

Picture: BMW Werkfoto, 1978/ BMW Archiv, 1998

calculation and sensing can take place, so that optimal ignition timing is always maintained."

With such microelectronics, there is nothing to wear out, as was the case for the original contact ignition systems, or any mechanical components. However, reprogramming the electronic brain is a time-consuming and expensive business, as many racing teams have found out both in Formula 1 (where BMW also used Bosch computer-processed engine management) and in sedan racing.

Detail production run changes

Following the 1978 debut of the 635, small but important changes took place at regular intervals.

From July 1979, bigger BMWs were available with a 12-function on-board computer. The 6 Series was a natural for such equipment, but the complexity of the anti-theft code button operation defeated even senior BMW employees over the years. The computer was and is useful, but became a lot more user-friendly when the E30 3 Series made it a servant rather than taskmaster from October 1982 onward.

Among 7 Series sedans, July 1979 was a significant date, one that was to enhance 6 Series handling appreciably. The turbocharged 745i did not lead to an equivalent 6 Series, but the *Doppelgelenk* (double linkage) front suspension would also be transferred (eventually) to the coupe cousins of the early eighties.

BMW stated that the main effect of the replacement front suspension was to "allow steering offset to be laid out over a widely variable range." For the customer, the most apparent bonus was improved front suspension location and consequently better improved communication with the driver.

At the rear, the European 1979 model year also debuted an anti-dive linkage that was to feature on 6 Series. The coupe's rear suspension could not be fundamentally improved until the 5 Series subsequently donated replacement trailing arm installation angles. Officially the coupes adopted the Five's better-mannered realigned trailing arm back suspension during the summer of 1982, making it part and parcel of every 635CSi with 3.4 liter power.

Extensive interior changes added to the driver information services offered, losing a tad on the original layout for style, but a model of clarity. The 1979 coupe took on a digital clock with red LED readout to replace the traditional analogue (with blower fan adjustment bezel) among deeper interior changes that were complete by summer 1982.

These saw the four spoke steering wheel and original instrumentation ditched in favor of three spoke wheel with fatter boss cladding and BMW's starkest and clearest black and white dials. An econometer was incorporated in the lower sector of the speedometer, and it was in 1982 that the Service Interval Indicator debuted on 6 Series. This was to prove a long-lived idea that spread service intervals according to usage (more short trips, more trips to the dealer) throughout the BMW range, and is in current use.

Back in 1979, we could see that changes arrived at different points for 6 Series, but wherever components could be made in common with the Seven or Five they usually were adopted for the flagship coupe. Exceptions included the vented rear discs of the coupes, which were not allowed to transfer back to even the most powerful 745 derivative of 140 mph capability.

Similarly, contemporary factory diagrams display that the second link on the front suspension of 7 Series did not become a production line reality on 6 Series until post-June 1981. The suspension changes had first to be engineered and adapted to 5 Series before there was an obvious path to the joint 5/6 platform.

In June 1979, it was also noticeable that some minor detailing work had gone on for the 635. A shallower back spoiler outline, the second rear

Inside the European specification 6 Series of the 1982 model year, we can see both the cloth front trim and the (usually optional) leather layout for the rear. Later European models (certainly post-1987) featured rear headrests. The center armrest folds down and the aperture is carefully carpeted.

Picture: BMW Archiv, 1984

The interior of the 1983 model year US specification 633CSi reveals the lack of 8-button test control from the European standard equipment lists and a three-spoke safety wheel masking the computer.

Picture: BMW NA, December 1983

spoiler design was color-coded to the body color and cleared the back Roundel badge, whereas the original carried the badge. Standard velour trims were adopted and central locking, controlled from the boot or the passenger door, appeared on the standard specification.

More importantly the 3.5 liter engine gained the Digital Motor Electronic system of those 3210 cc pioneers in autumn of 1980. The 633CSi was still available in the UK with automatic ZF transmission at £17,462 but this was the last year in Britain for the 633, which would sell on in the US until replaced by the 635 for 1985 model year.

The demise of 633CSi in 1980 UK left a choice of 628 and 635CSi models that prevailed until 1984, when the first of the M-coupes joined the RHD line. The 628 lasted until 1987 in Britain—it was never exported to the USA—and was manufactured as an introduction to the coupe line in Europe until May 1988. The 628CSi was nearly the most unpopular of all Sixers; only the original 630CS joined it in a sub-6000 production run.

The next chapter examines the most successful sports and commercial coupe of the breed, the 3.4 liter for Europe and America.

This is the later European-specification, 3.4 liter motor. It shared some intake manifold castings with the 3.2 liter used in the 633CSi.

Picture: David Shepherd, 1998

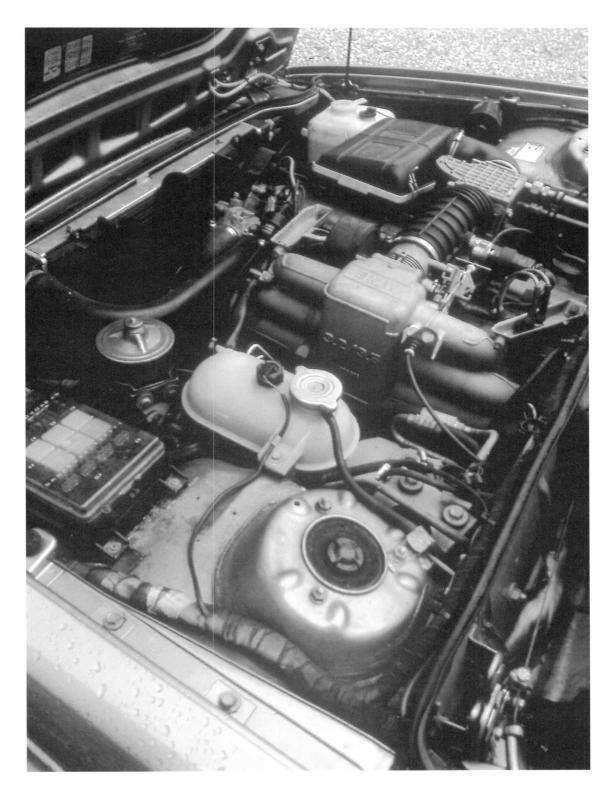

QUICK FACTS

Product

3.4 liter inline six was part of a long-lived range generically coded M30 and nicknamed "Big Six"

Made

The 3.4 liter variant lasted 1982–89 (Europe); 1984–89 (US) for 6 Series, but also for many other BMWs.

Production

M30 only, a total of 1,415,729 of the single overhead camshaft sixes of 2.5 to 3.5 liters were made between 1968 and 1994

Performance

(3.4 liter): 218 bhp @ 5200 rpm with 224 lb ft at 4000 rpm (Europe). US Federal, 182 bhp @ 5400 rpm and 214 lb-ft by 4000 rpm.

Brave Heart

How the faithful single camshaft six cylinder (M30) was slimmed down and toned up for toughness over bigger mileages. What was the big deal? We tell you.

Summer of 1982, Munich. Hans Erdman Schönbeck, BMW sales director, and original Flying Finn motor rally winner Rauno Aaltonen spoke persuasively in Munich of the next step in the coupe's progress. The grayhaired Schönbeck, resplendent in an immaculate blue blazer, addressed us at an international press presentation held in part of the BMW executive canteen, "Welcome to the totally revised BMW 6 Series, the second generation of the BMW coupes first introduced in 1976. Approximately 35,000 vehicles of this series have rolled off the assembly lines so far, a high figure for this class of automobiles."

Externally there was little sign of the considerable mechanical and weight-saving change that had been made. Just a new front apron and closed bottom to the engine compartment betrayed that BMW as becoming more concerned with aerodynamics, while the rear bumper was extended to provide better protection at the sides.

Standard wheel sizes became 6.5 J x 14 inch with 205/70VR tires on their alloy rims. British 635s, and those for many major markets, will be more familiar on the multi-spoke and odd-sized alloy rims that support Michelin TRX 220/50 VR 390 (15.35 inch diameter) low profile and steel-braced rubber.

Those with really sharp eyes could peer at the headlamps and note a stepped reflector dividing the lamp with a lower half to provide better side and short distance "fill-in" illumination. Fog lamps were integrated with the front end panels (which followed the Seven in offering a generally softer, flowing interpretation of the original Bracq Turbo-

One of BMW's best press handout pictures, ever: the 1984 model year 635CSi at winter play. How did they keep it *that* clean between photographic runs?

Picture: BMW Werkfoto, 1984

inspired shape) and at the rear, high intensity fog warning lights became production items too.

Internally, the weight reduction progress was a spectacular average of 132 lbs (60 kg). The body could now be further lightened in line with the later steel technology and the prevailing crash test standards, rather than those anticipated at the design stages. A curb weight of 1430 kg was given for both models, contrasting with 1500 kg originally claimed for 635 and 1450 kg for 628CSi.

The chassis was totally overhauled. BMW engineers had been forced to wait for some 7 Series components, like the full double link front suspension with reduced steering roller radius, and the 1981 5 Series debutante, a relocated steering trailing arm angle of 13 degrees with its articulated overhead linkage placed behind the axle line.

Since the 5 Series had adopted such features in 1981—although the remounted trailing arms were initially confined to performance derivatives such as the 528i—it was logical that the coupes should also benefit from a layout designed to cope with bumps, puddles and tire deflation with minimum front end drama.

A rear layout change tidied up the BMW's manners in a tail-slide, and also made such excess throttle skids unlikely on a dry road with the broader TRX 50 per cent aspect ratio tires installed. Net result? A far more roadworthy car with far less reaction to sudden bursts on the throttle, or sharp deceleration.

Most 1982 facelift 635s left the Dingolfing production lines with this unique 15.35-inch diameter alloy and 220/50 VR 390 Michelins specifically developed as original equipment for the 635 BMW. The author's car (seen here) uses half-price British Avon Turbospeeds to the same dimensions in all but their 55 percent profiles.

Picture: Author, January 1998

In the European Sixer's summer of 1982 modifications the 635 truly became the 634, and it emerged that BMW had suffered a service problem with the previous Motorsport-inspired 3453 cc engine and its 93.4 mm bore. So they reworked the faithful slant six into yet another permutation, allying a 92 mm bore with the 3210 cc's stroke of 86mm to produce a European 6 and 7 Series 3.5 liter power unit used beneath 635/735 badges.

Tight fit. The 3.4-liter single overhead camshaft six does not look glamorous in this engineering picture of its installation, which clearly shows how much of its mass was carried in front of the axle line. Note how close the fan and distributor are to the front radiator: it is not unknown for fan and radiator to come into contact as mileage mounts and mountings soften!

Picture: BMW Archiv, 1998

It displaced 3430 cc and European power was quoted as the same 218 bhp at 5200 rpm with an unchanged torque peak.

Engine detail work for the 3.4 liter newcomer comprised an increase in compression from the old 3.5 liter's 9.3:1 to 10:1. BMW utilized a second stage in Digital Motor Electronics which added a fuel mixture graph to that of the ignition. It was augmented, via another mapping session, specifically to control the warm-up through the cold start phase. In the search for improved fuel consumption, even the idling speed was knocked back 50 rpm and the fuel shut-off point on over-run was shifted to 1000 rpm.

The later 3430 cc engine was mated as standard with an overdrive five speed gearbox which achieved 13–15 percent quoted consumption savings, in conjunction with lowered weight and idling speed reduction. Rpm-reduction may not have sounded much at 50 revs but BMW asserted, "nearly two thirds of this 13–15 percent success are thanks to the reduced idling speed".

US specifications

That was the story in Europe, but for the US the dimensionally identical 3430 cc was worked hard to meet emission requirements and dropped to a shadow of its original 635 performance when asked to shift the heavier US model. A three-way catalytic converter and a sharply reduced compression ratio of 8:1 (replacing 10:1) told us not to expect much. The Federal version, burning unleaded gas, made 36 horsepower and 10 lb-ft of torque less than in Europe.

The 635CSi finally hit the streets in time for the autumn 1984 magazines to publish an American 635CSi specification, one that lasted only until February 1987. The need to sell the M6 as the performer in the range led to the usual high grade 635 features being offered as the L6 alternative.

The L6 name did not sell, and the 635CSi badge was also used from 1988 onward. Even though the Federal 635 died on the production lines with the European derivatives (April 1989), I do hold US reports of sales continuing into the early nineties; see appendices. By then the 850i had made the transatlantic trip and 1991 was to be the 8 Series' best manufacturing year.

Standard 1985 US 635CSi equipment paired to the 209 cubic inch/3.4 liter six was significant for the introduction of standard ABS braking. As one US independent sourly commented at the time, this was a full 20 years after the first European developments of ABS (Dunlop had an erratic but safe system for a few hundred Chrysler V8 Jensen Interceptor 4x4 coupes in the early sixties) and seven painful years after such electronically-processed anti-lock braking became a commonplace production feature from Mercedes, BMW and Porsche.

For magazine tests and standard official import specification, the 635CSi was offered with the Getrag five speed gearbox, but it did not win friends for its "notchy" shift action. Most customers opted for the $795 option of a ZF four speed auto. When the L6 hit the US market alongside the M6, BMW NA specified it have a standard four speed ZF automatic transmission that was electronically managed.

Any of the Federal 635s delivered in the snowline States should wear an optional $390 limited slip differential, otherwise traction is truly appalling over snow and ice. Incidentally the rear end ratio for the US was 3.45:1, whereas 3.07:1 was the European 635 norm.

All US 635s were initially specified with air conditioning, power-adjusted leather seats (no cloth option), trip computer and unique Michelin forged aluminum wheels. These were sized 6.5 x 15.4 inches to support showroom 220/55VR 390 rubber, generously plump by the standard

Showing all of the changes made since its 1976 debut, the 6 Series cockpit (this is a European 635CSi) features no central clock, as the 3-lever and rotary heating/ventilation controls occupy that site. On this computer-equipped model, the computer readout defaults to time and date. Instrumentation changed subtly in the early 1980s as well, featuring a rectangular minor dial for fuel contents and water temperature, locat ed between the electronically activated speedometer and the 6,400-rpm-redline tachometer.

Picture: BMW Werkfoto, 1982

equipment standards of the mid-eighties. However, the official import specification for a US 635CSi lacked the European rear spoiler and gained the ungainly extended bumpers.

The author has a suspicion that not all the lower-riding 635 suspension settings made it across the Atlantic. The steering wheel shown for the 1986 US model was a superior item to the production European wheel, equivalent to a more expensive BMW Motorsport specification, down to the detail stripes.

The revised Sixes were promptly (unusual by normal standards) phased into the right-hand drive (RHD) schedule and arrived in the UK in June 1982. They also sported ABS antilock braking, on-board computer, the Service Interval Indicator and a modified interior that featured a three spoke steering wheel and a three lever, thermostatically operated heating and ventilation system.

The new LCD readout of the digital clock was lower down the fascia and the instrumentation behind the traditional single pane was considerably altered. The same speed, rpm, water temperature and fuel contents were monitored by dials, but the style was new. Now, the speedometer incorporated a fuel economy indicator that was electrically connected, rather than the notoriously inaccurate vacuum manifold "econometers" beloved of mass manufacturers.

Pricing

For the American market a cost of more than $41,000 in its first year ($43,075 in 1986, with Gas Guzzler penalty), put the BMW firmly in the luxury coupe class. It looked expensive against a Jaguar XJ-S V12 (up around $50000), but a bargain against a 560SEC Mercedes. BMW's ultimate German rival demanded up to $20,000 more for their much more powerful (by 56 bhp) V8 coupe, yet the media performance statistics for BMW's six cylinder manual transmission 635 were hardly humiliated by the automatic transmission-only Benz.

Interiors grew even more luxurious, particularly in the US showroom specification. Here is the 1988 model year European 635CSi with napa leather and the three-position memory seats that were standardized in the US.

Picture: BMW Werkfoto, 1987

The stunning Alpina B7S version of the BMW 635 coupe featured KKK turbo-charging and an intercooler in front of the main water radiator. A hand-wheel-adjusted boost control from the cockpit released 250 to 330 ps by 5,800 rpm, with a weighty 377 lb-ft of torque at just 2,400 rpm. It went like a missile, but always with distinctly non-military finesse.

Picture: Alpina GmbH/
Buchloe, 1982

The Sixer was some $10,000 under the tag for a Porsche 928, but the Porsche had 100 bhp more from its V8 and BMW once again took some body blows from the press for lack of grunt per dollar spent. Such US complaints had been evident for the older Federal 633CSi (then phased out).

Since the 635 offered just about 1 bhp more than a late model 633CSi delivered, all in a curb weight measured some 100 lbs up on its American market predecessor. It was no wonder that many European 'Gray Import' specification 635s arrived outside the BMW NA official network. These pulled in at US ports with the full 218 bhp Euro output.

UK introductory prices were £16,635 and £22,950: some two years later the tags read £19,275 for 628 and £24,995 for big brother, which sold at £36,860 for the 1987–90 sales years. So it's always best in Britain to get on and purchase a BMW as soon as finance allows, rather than waiting around for the virtually unknown price drop or discount special. Even at that sky high UK price for the 635 it is worth noting that air conditioning was a £1374 option in 1984, or a £1212 luxury on the 628 of 1980.

Proven Performance

Because of the minimal horsepower gains made in Federal form over the 633, the heavier 635 was pushed to show any real US performance advantage over its predecessor in standing start acceleration runs over the 0-30 or 0–60 mph span. Expect the 5-speed manual 635CSi to gallop from rest to 30 mph in some 2.5 seconds, or slip closer to 8 than 8.5 seconds on the rumble from 0–60 mph.

For a then universally illegal (in US) standing start launch into the 100 mph zone, the torquier 635 did show some seconds gain over the Federal 633, averaging out around three seconds. Top speed was reported as 131 mph by *Road & Track*, 132 mph for *Car & Driver* with 17 to 17.5 US mpg independently returned.

European performance of these "second generation" 6 Series was much as before but fuel consumption could be substantially changed by the transmission specification. In Britain, the 635 was sold with no extra cost alternatives of ZF's latest "switchable" four speed automatic gearbox, or the standard OD five speeder, or the quintuplet, direct top, close ratio cluster.

On the manual transmission front that meant BMW quoted an average of 26.6 Imperial mpg for the OD five speed-equipped car, 24.5 mpg with the sportier gear set, or 24.45 mpg in automatic transmission trim. That latter figure could be further modified by quoting the figures in the Sport or Economy modes of the ZF automatic box, but I think we've got enough figures without resorting to pedantic dirty tricks...

More everyday relevance can be obtained from *Motor*'s overall 22.5 mpg for a manual 635 of July 1982 which had managed an observed 137.1 mph and 0–60 in a fine 6.9 seconds. The same weekly British magazine also tried the 628 CSi but in 1980, and reported a 130 mph maximum for the 184 bhp harnessed in 3197 lb (1453 kg). *Motor* also ran 0–60 mph in 8.3 seconds, plus 19.8 mpg overall on leaded 97 octane gas.

Autocar's European 635CSi figures were available to fit later, and reported 139 mph, 0–60 in 7.3 seconds and an average 21.8 mpg. Like the author, they had not experienced a 628 CSi. Incidentally, UK availability of automatic transmissions included arrival of the four speed unit with its fuel-saving tall top gear in January 1983, and the switchable unit a year later. Important later eighties changes for 635 included a significantly

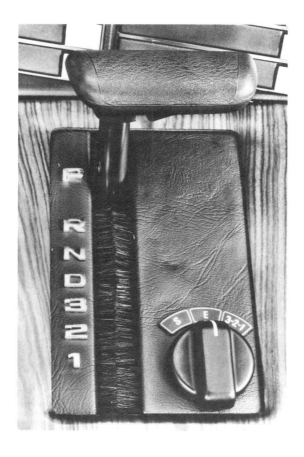

The split-personality ZF automatic gearbox provided sport, economy, and individual gear hold (1–2–3) modes from the right-hand rotary switch. A no-cost option in some major 1983–84 European markets, it allowed the 635 a tall (overdriven for 32 mph per 1,000 rpm) top gear for premium economy, and lost surprisingly little acceleration. Key figures for the European 635 auto included a 135 mph maximum, 0–60 mph in 7.5 seconds, and an average 20 mpg in hard use.

Picture: BMW GB, 1984

Smarter. By the fall of 1987, the European engine specification for the 635CSi changed considerably with the adoption of an engine it shared with its 735i brother, which had learned to live with lower-octane unleaded fuel, tighter European exhaust emissions, and (for some markets) a European catalytic converter. It featured a replacement cylinder head with lowered (9.2:1) compression and Bosch Motronic microprocessor engine management.

Official power output was 220 bhp, slightly up on the previous 3.4-liters, but independent test times in automatic trim were slower than before—down around 8.5 seconds for 0–60 mph . Maximum speed in Europe trim measured out a sliver under 135 mph and fuel economy was down by 2 mpg.

Picture: BMW Werkfoto, 1987

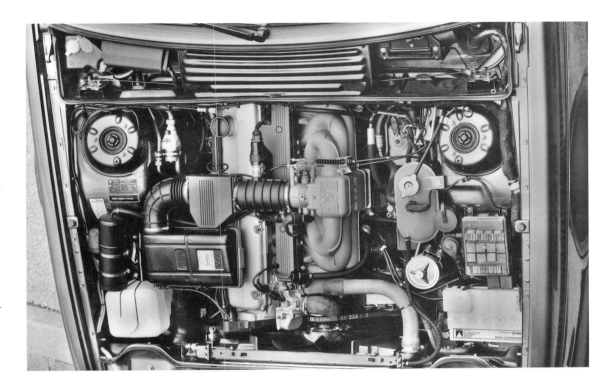

modified motor, climate control air conditioning and uprated headlamps in the Autumn of 1987 and automatic ride height control for the rear suspension a year later.

Most important of the engine changes was not the additional 2 bhp (now 220 at 5700 rpm) but the fact that BMW had rationalized European 6 Series specifications with those of the 735i. That meant that the 3430 cc wore later Bosch Digital Motor Electronics and a replacement cylinder head. The latter dropped compression back to 9.2:1 and could run unleaded gas with no changes required: my 1986 model runs either 97 octane leaded or (much more expensive in Europe) 98 octane super unleaded.

Tested in 1988 by London's *Autocar*, it was revealed that maximum torque had also been augmented (up 4 lb-ft to 232 lb-ft by an unchanged 4000 rpm). Then in its twelfth production year, the revised 635CSi gave less appealing performance on a replacement 3.64:1 final drive: fuel consumption was measured at 17.2 mpg, 0–60 mph occupied 8.4 automatic transmission seconds (0–100 took 21.5 seconds) and it topped out at 134 mph.

All these figures were not so effective as a 1982 automatic 635 tested by the same magazine, 0–60 mph some 1.1 seconds longer, top speed down a

The Federal version of the 635 motor gave 36 bhp less than its European cousins, but remained strong on mid-range torque.

Picture: BMW NA, supplied 1998

couple of mph and fuel consumption (leaded gas and high compression in the earlier CSi) more than 2 mpg better overall (19.7 mpg in 1982). So there is a price for apparent progress, but I confess I would prefer the later model for its cheaper unleaded fuel capability and detail specification enhancements on my home market.

Figure talk

Production rates did increase for the European line of the 628/635. The mainly US-bound 633CSi also fared better in the eighties, although another 62 units in 1983 would have been needed to match 633CSi's peak in serving all main markets with 3387 copies during 1978.

The 635 proved the big seller in Europe, as well as giving BMW Motorsport a basis on which to support saloon car racing with a current coupe, after seasons of backing the obsolete Karmann CSL coupes of 1968–75.

Alpina *haute couture.*
Our tribute to the man
behind the 166-mph
street 6 Series includes
the man himself:
Burkard Bovensiepen
with one of his fabu-
lous engines taking
shape at the Buchloe
base.

Then, a cockpit shot to
let you know that
Alpina left little
untouched in their
thorough factory
assembly of a con-
verted coupe; aside
from the obvious four-
spoke steering wheel,
there was a line of
subsidiary instru-
ments (including a
turbocharger boost
gauge), and even the
186 mph (300 km/h)
speedometer carried
the Alpina logo.

Pictures: Author,
June 1982

In its first year, the 635 sold 1286 and the following 1979 season brought 3775 sales. That was a record exceeded in 1982 with the aid of the new model (4148) and nearly matched for 1983 with some 3668 sold. This compared with 3324 of the 633CSi and only 972 of the 628 in the same year, a total of 7970 BMW 6 Series manufactured in 1983. In 1982 they made an overall 7593, well up on the depressed 5652 of 1981, one of the lowest figures for 6 Series production that BMW reported until the final year's 1064 in 1989.

"Number crunching" a little further (aided by Richard Feast, then of *Automotive News*, and the German *Verband Der Automobilindustrie, VDA*)

Driving right on to the end of the run, the 635CSi and its 6 Series brothers. They proved an impossible act to replace commercially by the vastly more expensive V12 BMW 850i.

Picture: BMW Werkfoto, 1982

The European chrome bumper specification stayed until 1987, when the (German-registered) example displayed a modified front end, together with Federal-style end-caps to the bumpers, which were color-coded in Europe.

Pictures: BMW Werkfoto, 1987; Author, 1998

we find that individual total coupe production to the close of 1983 stacked up as follows. The champion, with 21,889 examples produced from 1976 to 1983, and the only survivor of the original range, was the 633CSi.

Then with just two seasons fewer in European production, and no initial US market, came the 635 with 19,087 produced. A year younger, but definitely the collector's choice on rarity value, was the 628CSi with 4173 made; even the 1979-buried 630CS had managed 5763.

Taking all models for a final grossing-up, we find BMW had made 50,912 in the seven years between 1976–83, handsomely putting to rest the 44,254 final figure for the preceding 1968–75 BMW coupe series. This also shaded what BMW would achieve (some 28,268) over a similar period with that sagging 6 Series successor, the 8 Series.

Final 6 Series production of 1976-89 passed 86,200 copies and the 635 alone exceeded the combined production output of all the 1965–75 coupes with 45,213 made in a run that spanned almost 11 years in Europe. The 635 coupe was badly delayed on its way to the US, so it was not surprising that just 13,008 (some 30 percent of the 635CSi total production) were manufactured to Federal emission specification between 1984–89. So

6 Series slumber in sunny California. A sample of the models attending Monterey 1996, at which BMW was the honored Marque.

Picture: Author California, 1996

the move to 6 Series sophistication was commercially justified in numbers, but only the sporting 635s and M6s credibly lent 140 mph muscle to the argument that they were faster machines than their ancestors.

From current perspective we can see that the 6 Series handsomely doubled sales of its charismatic forerunners, and the Sixer also made an impossible act for the 8 Series to follow, a curious fact of nineties life that I explore in chapter 10. Suffice it here to say that the 8 Series only twice looked like matching 6 Series annual output, and that was back in 1990/1. Thereafter, annual 8 Series output figures were regularly half or a third that of 6 Series.

Now let's look at the beefiest production BMW 6 Series of them all: M635i for Europe, M6 stateside.

QUICK FACTS

Production

October 1984 to February 1989 (US-specification)
November 1986 to September 1988.

Production

5855 (1767 to US specification)

Performance

Maximum speed 155 mph (145 mph); 0–60 mph 6
seconds (6.8 sec); 0–100 mph 15.5 seconds (17 seconds). Fuel consumption: 17.5 UK mpg (15.5 US)

People

"Prophet" Csaba Csere of *Car & Driver* magazine,
Georg Thiele (S38 motor engineer), Werner
Frohwein (chassis uprates)

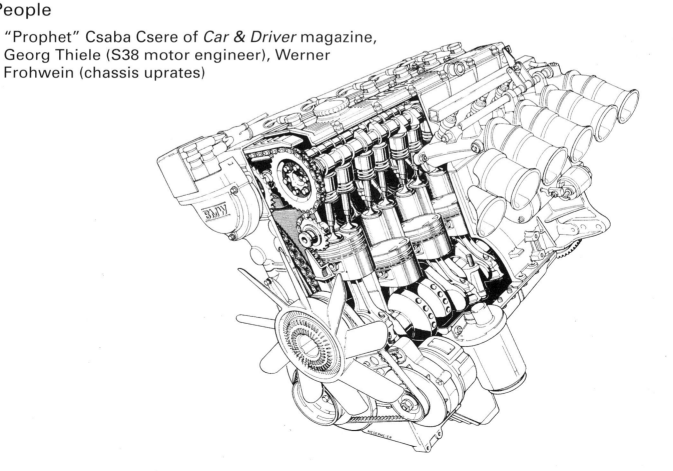

M-Powerhouse

The ultimate production Six ran with 24-valve
vigor, thrilled its owners but never found
a race track home

"The M635CSi is many things all rolled into one without being a compromise: an elegant classical coupe combined with an intriguing extra margin of performance and pure driving pleasure." That is how BMW in Munich saw the M-coupe when sales had begun in Spring 1984. Then the price was 89,500 Dm, or a quoted $31,450 and £23,300 when the American and British press took German preview drives in 1984.

Sales were then expected to reach beyond the 1000 mark, instead of the originally planned 400. Between April 1984 and the February 1989 termination, total manufacture of these very special Sixes with S38-coded 24 valve power reached 5855. Of these, 1767 (made between November 1986 and September 1988) were officially destined for the US with 256 bhp rather than the European 286 horsepower rating.

Why the American market delay?

Initially I think there were two reasons: first, no perceived profit in marketing a more muscular 635 for the US market; second, bottlenecks in BMW engineering resources to produce an emissions-certified variant tailored to US regulations.

Researching these points uncovered an uncanny prophecy from *Car & Driver*'s Csaba Csere. The American monthly magazine writer introduced his July 1984 preview piece on the M635CSi, "James Bond would feel right at home in a BMW 635CSi. Emergencies in the Balkans would be in easy reach of the motorway-gobbling big coupe. Those Alpine-switchback

games of tag with the sinister forces of SPECTRE would be easy sport for
the BMW's acceleration and handling, even with a full compliment of Q's
death-dealing devices in the ample trunk.

"More critical yet to 007 than mere life and death, the Bavarian coupe
has the proper blend of racy lines and understated elegance for whisking
luscious double agents away from the baccarat tables of Monte Carlo." I
hope Csaba Csere is now sitting beside his LA pool, multiple phone lines
fully occupied counting the movie cash mountain that accompanied his
decade-early prediction of the BMW-Bond alliance. Perhaps Csere is now
making the new Bond deals to follow the Pierce Brosnan Bond BMWs of
the mid-nineties featured in the epics *Goldeneye* and *Tomorrow Never Dies*
which premiered the Z3 in advance of production and featured both
BMW two and four wheel products in the follow-up.

Sales plans for M635 in the US were originally denied in 1984, especially as it was that year that the 182 bhp Federal 635CSi debuted. The
advent of gray imports and continuous pressure to uprate the image of
the 6 Series line led to a belated change of heart in Munich. The US got
the re-badged and emission-engineered M635CSi as the M6 from Feb-

Standard European
trim looked pretty
basic with all cloth
seating, although
adjustment was com-
prehensive, as can be
seen from the double
levers and rotary knob
(closest to camera).
The official US specifi-
cation included leather
trim with power-
adjustable 3-memory
seats.

Picture: BMW Werkfoto,
1983

ruary 1987 onward. It lasted but two model years, initially alongside the
automatic transmission, 12-valve 635, which was redesignated L6 to
emphasize their differences.

BMW factory records show that—of a total 1767—just 255 of the US-
specification M6s were manufactured in November and December 1986.
These rarities were followed by 1193 examples in 1987 and 319 for the
nine months of E24 production devoted to the US M6 in 1989.

Those years of delay before BMW's flagship coupe arrived in America
cost potential customers dearly. Prices almost doubled from the 1984 prediction, so that when *Motor Trend* tried the M6 on California turf the tag
read $58,200 including more than $2200 in Gas Guzzler taxes. That was
without major extras. To be fair, the showroom specification was extensive
and embraced air conditioning with a sunroof, outstanding leather cabin
finish, including power seats with three-driver position memory, a limited
slip differential and eight-speaker AM/FM stereo.

US buyers were short-changed on power compared to Europe, the official M6 import (and there were plenty which came in unofficially at European power levels) was some 30 bhp or 12 percent down on the M635CSi.

Ready to install, a 24-valve straight six displays the complex exhaust system plumbing that was developed extensively for a 30° slant six rather than the original vertical stance.

Picture: BMW Werkfoto, 1983

Interconnecting those individual butterfly throttles was a carefully crafted, ball-jointed throttle linkage.

Picture: BMW Werkfoto, 1983

As installed in the
M635CSi for Europe,
the 3453-cc motor filled
the front engine bay
with MPower muscular-
ity. Note the external
water passage rail run-
ning above the exhaust
maze.

Picture: BMW Werkfoto,
1983

The start point for the
M6/M635CSi engine
development was the
mechanically injected,
dry-sump M1 motor.
Here, we see that mid-
mounted installation,
the engine upright
ahead of the rear 5-
speed transaxle. Make
no mistake, the M1
was—and remains—a
fabulous street-driving
experience, but the
electronically managed
M6 was even better,
and boasted another 9
horsepower.

Picture: BMW Werkfoto,
1978

The M-cockpit featured
the leather-rim, three-
spoke steering wheel
and the M-badge upon
the 6,900-rpm-redlined
tachometer.

Picture: BMW AG,
originated 1983/BMW
Archiv, reprinted 1998

However, the lower compression DOHC 24-valver (9.8:1 versus Europe's 10.5:1) with its more restrictive exhaust still made 256 bhp and 243 lb-ft of torque (the Euro statistic was 251 lb-ft).

The US-bound result was still capable of clipping 0–60 mph in a shade under 7 seconds and 0–100 mph in comfortably under 20 seconds with a maximum speed (usually calculated by American independents) of some 145 mph.

That was enough to satisfy the testers, and they might have been glad to learn that BMW NA usually sets the most competitive prices of BMW's major markets. For example, in Britain they often paid in pounds the US price in dollars, meaning up to double, dependent on exchange rates and model. European markets of the period usually set a low base price and charged heavily for any "extras" including a radio!

The only major dynamic complaint voiced by US testers was the rate at which the M6 consumed gas (averaging 15.5 US mpg), not because of the price but the limited range offered by the 16.6 gallon tank. Some of the California runs into the desert scrublands called for restraint, if you were to reach 200 miles a tankful.

British supplies of the M635 were scheduled for February 1985 in RHD at £33,750. The cost of RHD and items like the wider wheels and tires that were German options, were all in the UK price. As in Germany, the pricing of Porsche's 310 bhp 928S was the guideline, but the M635 swiftly escalated from its German equivalent of £23,300 in 1984 to surpass £33,000 on arrival in 1985 Britain and reached £45,780 by 1986. Just about 10 percent of all M635s manufactured (524) had right-hand drive steering, but even at its eye-watering £40,000 plus in 1986 (a Jaguar XJ-S V12 was just £26,300 on its home market!) the M-coupe built a loyal following. The RHD batch was the last down the line in a 52-off batch of early 1989.

Birth of M-Power coded S38

From a simple T-shirt logo, to the side of Nelson Piquet's World Championship Brabham-BMWs, the M-Power legend was conscientiously promoted by BMW. A coupe expression of that philosophy was the six inline cylinders with double overhead camshafts and 24 valves to pro-

During his reign as the first man to win the FIA Formula 1 World Championship in a turbocharged car, Brazil's Nelson Piquet took delivery of a very special M6. This is Brabham-BMW driver Piquet with an M-coupe, but this is not his all-black special of August 1984. His example—presented during the Hockenheim German Grand Prix of 1984—had an oversized motor (3.7 liters) that developed 330 street horsepower and was said to nuzzle 170 mph.

Picture: BMW GB, reprinted 1984

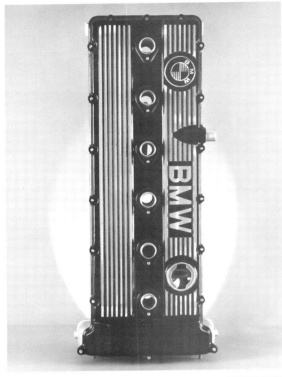

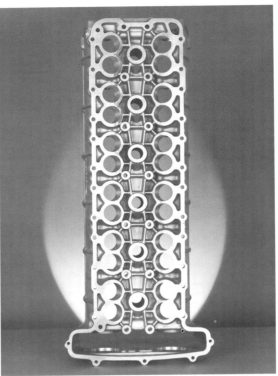

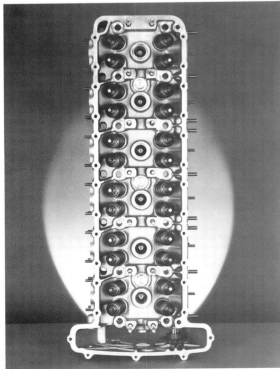

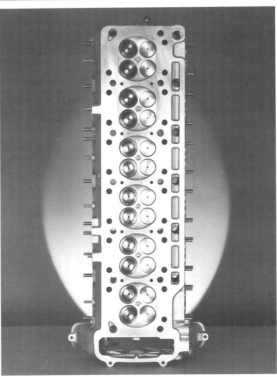

This composite quartet shows us the first of BMW's ever more stylish cast rocker covers (top right) alongside the classic pentroof, central-spark-plug layout of the quad-valve-per-cylinder combustion chambers (bottom right).

The timing case houses twin overhead camshafts, each with bearings, plus accommodation for the lower maintenance tappets (top and bottom left). The lower section of the cylinder head reveals the 38 degree v-pattern disposition of 24 valves (bottom right).

Pictures: BMW Werkfoto, 1983

vide an independently timed 150 mph, 0–60mph acceleration in 6.5 seconds, and a standing quarter mile in 15.1 seconds with a top speed of 95.7 mph. In other words a 6 Series that "moved" with a capital M, while still providing 19 UK mpg in the hands of *Performance Car*, the UK monthly magazine that presented those typical fifth wheel test figures after lugging all their Correvit electronic test gear to Germany to test the M635 while still in its LHD-only infancy. Other European testers, who got a longer run on measuring maximum speed, came closer to 155 of the 158 mph claimed by BMW.

Although BMW Motorsport also uprated every other component needed to compliment such stirring performance—brakes, suspension, transmission and interior—the key was that magnificent motor, which was shared by the E28 sedan M5 Series in production from October 1984 to November 1987. Some 600 M5s of the E28 breed were officially allocated to the US at $43,500 each but Munich shipped 82 such cars in 1986 and 1288 before US production ceased at 1370 examples in November 1987, most sold as 1988 models.

The M5 took on many subsequent E34 body guises and stretched the 24-valve big six concept to its ultimate 3.8 liters/340 bhp before production of the E34 sedan and touring M5 bodies ceased in July 1995. There was then a production gap in Munich's M5 output and the straight six never made it back to the line; today's M5 is V8-powered.

I was privileged to talk with Georg Thiele in 1984, when the M635 was beginning to make an impact on Germany's Autobahns. We met at at BMW Motosport Preussentrasse headquarters, then the most presentable sports emporium the writer had seen in 17 years of nosing around, or working within, major manufacturers' competition departments. There was a large showroom to the street front, but behind lurked a quadrangle of assembly workshops and test cells that made BMW Motosport a miniaturized version of the parent company.

It was and is not just a one floor deal, either. Below you found the tentacles of Paul Rosche's engine empire with safe-like steel doors and testing equipment that can run any engine up to GP power level through a complete race track simulation, or a simple airflow cylinder head test, as required.

Above the ground floor are offices of all kinds, housing heavier and heavier engineering talent to the back of the quadrangle, and administrations, then including Rennleiter (race leader) Dieter Stappert, above the street front.

In pursuit of M635 knowledge, I interviewed the engineer responsible for the practicalities of a 24-valve engine program that was initiated in

1980. Georg Thiele had a lot of existing knowledge to draw on in developing the 3.5 liter six a stage further: competition experience with the older 24-valve racing coupe, refinement of the 470 bhp M1 mid-engined competitors plus street use of the M1 in its 277 bhp rating.

For M5/M6 deployment, there were some important advances in driving manners and fuel economy that engine management systems would make possible for the fabled Six. There was also the requirement to install the motor at the traditional BMW sedan car slant of 30 degrees, rather than vertically, as in M1, or the race cars , which had dry sump lubrication. Installing the six cylinder car's individually lengthy exhaust pipes at the critically correct lengths within a sedan engine bay took up much development time.

The basic starting point was a 3453 cc BMW six (93.4 mm bore x 84 mm stroke) that came from Motorsport originally and that served on the road and track for the M1 and the 635CSi before the Summer 1982 reduction to 3.4 liters (92 x 86 mm). That meant items like the basic 635/M1 bottom end, with an immensely tough forged steel crankshaft were inbuilt from the start. However, note that the M1 employed race-style dry sump lubrication, not the usual roadgoing wet sump system that M635/M5 employed.

"Fuel economy and good town driving manners were very important in our development program," reported Herr Thiele with a gentle smile, bravely struggling with the unfamiliar use of English, or my patchy German, before he outlined the detail work that turned the 277 bhp of the M1 into a more refined 286 horsepower for the M635. The later six also developing 250 lb-ft of torque at 4500 rpm instead of M1's 244 lb-ft at a more peaky 5000 revs.

The street transformation principles were the same as when Paul Rosche and the team turned the four valve per cylinder six from the earlier coupe's racing power plant into a unit for the M1 that could be used on the street.

Georg Thiele declared, "valve sizes are the same—37 mm inlet and 32 mm exhaust—and the camshafts are of [the] 264 degree duration that Rosche made for M1 - but we have made some important new parts. The cylinder head is the same casting, but with modifications to the waterways and inlet tracts to suit the 30 degree mounting. The waterways are no bigger than before, but they work with an inlet system that is now angled to suit the slanted engine.

"The way in which we arrange the tappets is completely new. Instead of the cap underneath, where everything must be taken apart to make an adjustment, we now have plates over the tappets, so you can make an

Using a far larger number of production ancillaries than its M1 forerunner, the 24-valve M6 unit weighed around 30 lbs. more than its 12-valve cousins. Overhead camshafts were driven by a single chain, whereas the M1 had a double-row chain and was built to rev at more than 7,000 rpm.

Drawing: Republished from a 1984 original

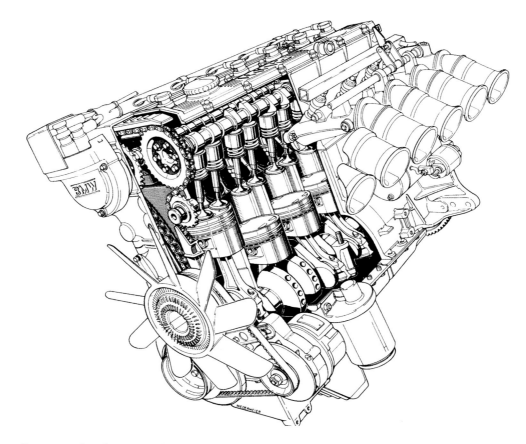

adjustment by changing the plate, because the tappet now works directly. Also the adjustment for the air flow in the fuel injection system is with a balance pipe and a central screw, instead of the awkward screws we had on M1," summarized Georg Thiele.

Indeed the single shaft and ball-joint throttle linkage were works of art. That linkage retained the individual throttle butterfly system of the road-going M1, rather than the single guillotine slide preferred in racing.

Statistically the biggest cylinder head change was revealed in the adoption of a fashionably high (10:5:1) compression in place of the M1's seventies levels of 9:1. The M635 gained its priority town manners and comparatively efficient fuel consumption from the use of Bosch ML-Jetronic injection and second generation Bosch Motronic engine management.

Maybe it was unglamorous to work on the lowest possible city idling speeds for such a glorious power unit, but Motronic and that revised injection with precision idling adjustment allowed Motorsport to match the close-ratio geared 635CSi on official fuel consumption figures with remarkable improvements at certain points.

The figures? At a constant 56 mph an M635 officially returned 36.2 UK mpg (7.8 L/100 kms) compared to the 12-valve coupe's 34.8 mpg (8.1 L/100 kms). At 75 mph both are dead equal at 29.1mpg (9.7 L/100 kms). Around town, there were only fractions between the 24-valve engine capable of 286 bhp and the 12-valve engine rated at 218 bhp: 17 mpg (16.6 L/100 kms) for the lowest power engine and 17.1 mpg (16.5 L/100 kms for the Autobahn-stormer!

If you looked at the graph Herr Thiele had on his wall, both the 635 and its M-coded bother recorded much the same consumption up to 100 mph, the Motorsport car drinking more heavily as it started to work harder to ultimately greater speeds. That was in stark contrast to the 745i turbo sedan, which had an awful fuel thirst as soon as any boost was needed, and generally posted rather more erratic fuel and power curves.

In American EPA test terms that meant the detail work on M635 brought the Munich missile into a range from 16 city use mpg to 22 US mpg on the highway. US and UK independent test results from a number of sources criticized the fuel consumption/fuel tank capacity and consequent safe driving range.

The lowest overall figure we have on record is 13.6 UK mpg at the test track, but a 1989 *Autocar* trial recorded 20.6 UK mpg for an example that also hit 0–60 mph in 6 seconds dead and topped out at 150 mph. In the US the best overall figures were around 17 mpg, but the average from three sources was below 16 mpg overall. By the way, all those US figures were for unleaded fuel and the lower compression engine, but the UK cars of the period ran leaded (98 octane) gas.

A 6-into-1 exhaust manifolding layout "took practically the whole time to make right, with good power, economy and to fit in the car," commented Herr Thiele wistfully. Other engine ancillaries were simplified considerably, compared with its mid-engined M1 ancestor.

For example the wet sump used the same pan and 6.5 liter capacity as a 218 horsepower 635. The oil and water pumps were the same as 635 and used the same belt system. The 80 amp/1120 watt alternator, viscous fan coupling, starter motor and single crankshaft damper were the same as for the slower production 6 Series.

Georg Thiele pointed out, "On the M1 it was necessary to have the double crankshaft damper for rpm over 7000. On this car there is a limiter for plus or minus (±) 100 rpm at 6900. Also we should say that the chain drive for the overhead camshafts is not the same as M1—that had

M is for Modified. Klaus
Schnitzer hovers above
the much-modified
engine bay of a 6 Series
coupe with carbureted
MPower and strut
brace bar.

Picture: Klaus Schnitzer
for *Roundel* magazine

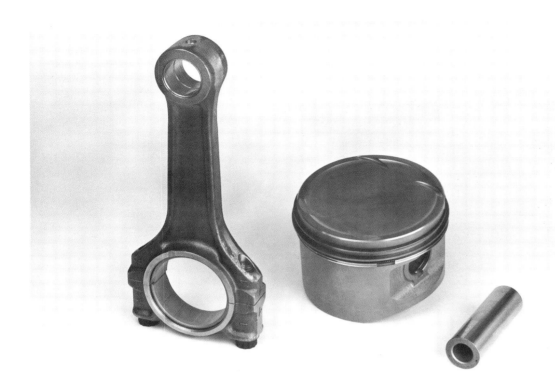

Elongated con rods and pistons shorter than than those used for the M1 were indicative of the changes involved in reworking the M1 motor into an M6 powerhouse. Note the valve recesses in the piston crowns and the enhanced oil control ring set.

Picture: BMW Werkfoto, 1983

a two-row Duplex chain, this one is a single row, smaller chain drive," explained Georg.

While assistants gallantly bore a complex cylinder head casting, complete with superbly crafted injection systems and linkages, Georg continued his detailed insight, explaining that the last translation of M-Power for a 6 Series was coded M88/3.

"The pistons and connecting rods were completely new, with the 3.5 liter engine's steel crankshaft. The pistons had different oil control rings: the M1 had them above the connecting rod bolt hole and now they are below. We have new piston crowns for the 10.5:1 compression, but also the cylinder bores have a special honing treatment. It is a special crosshatch treatment for good oil consumption and lubrication control and high rpm. It is not on the 2 valve per cylinder engine of 635, just for this M-car." A similar process was used on the bores of the Grand Prix racing turbo 4-cylinders.

You would think that this complex powerhouse would exact a painful weight penalty, but Georg Thiele reported, that it was "just 15 kg" more than the usual 635 motor, about 33 lbs. On the road in European trim the

Wearing the usual BMW North American publicity-conscious front plate, "The Ultimate Driving Machine," the 633CSi had much to live up to in the US. Straight-line performance was never going to be heroic with Federal emissions standards and 1980s technology. Sales exceeded 10,000 units, as it was the backbone of the US sales effort for BMW's biggest coupe of the period.

Picture: BMW NA,
October 1983

Then we have the glorious B7S in its dark green and gold livery (on the company's own alloy wheel design) alongside the 1982 635CSi press car.

Picture: Author,
June 1982

Unique double. Accompanied by co-researcher Peter Newton, I was able to drive the 1982 launch version of the BMW factory's 634CSi with 218 bhp, back-to-back with Alpina's fabulous B7S turbo derivative in Bavaria. The Alpina car had cockpit-adjustable boost and provided up to 330 horsepower! Acceleration from 0–60 mph was rated 5.9 seconds and at least a 166-mph maximum was expected.

Picture: Author, June 1982

Class act. In the fall of 1984, the 3.4-liter Federal 635CSi arrived in the US for the 1985 model year, complete with 5-mph enlarged bumpers of the kind worn by its predecessors. It brought most of the European features across the Atlantic, with the obvious exception of a rear spoiler. This point marked the standard introduction of ABS (anti-lock braking system) in the US for this model line.

Picture: BMW NA, 1984

At rest in the mountains, the Federal 635CSi gives its 182 bhp a rest: the ten-percent bonus in torque was welcome after the 633CSi. Big bumpers, extra weight, and the absence of some power offered to Europeans hit all 6-series particularly hard in US comparison tests versus Mercedes and Jaguar.

Picture BMW NA, 1984

Superb multi-spoke BBS wheels offered up to 9.5 inches of tread width. US showroom equipment for the fall of 1987 brought a price tag of almost $60,000 included these 16.3-inch diameter wheels with rim widths equivalent to 8 inches, as well as 240/45 VR415 Michelin TRX tires.

Picture: Courtesy BMW NA, originated 1986

As the logical alternative to the M6 branding (only used in the US), BMW NA offered this L6 luxury version of the 635. It was listed during 1987–90 and more than 5,157 were sold (we cannot be more precise, as all 6-series sales statistics were amalgamated after the 850's US introduction).

Picture: Courtesy BMW NA, 1987

The M6 in all its US glory, and this time they made sure the thing had a rear spoiler from the start! Some 1,767 examples of the Federal M6 with its 256-horsepower version of the 24-valve motor were officially imported between November 1986 and September 1988, but many more came into the US as Gray Imports in 286-bhp European specification.

Picture: Courtesy BMW NA, originated 1986

Usually referred to as a slow seller, the L6 variant of the Federal US 6-series differentiated a 12-valve 635 with standard luxury features versus the 24-valve M6's sportier specification. This is the facelifted 1987 model with black plastic cappings on the chrome bumpers.

The L6 actually outsold the 635 and M6, and 5,157 (minimum) were delivered. After 1990, L6 sales were lumped in with its stablemate in the US, the 850 introduced in 1991. However, Sixers continued to trickle out of US showrooms in 1991 and 1992 at the rate of 12 and 5, respectively, per year!

Picture: BMW NA
Released 1987

"The body beautiful" still attracts favorable bystander comment ten years after its production demise.

Picture: David Shepherd, 1998

The author's 1986 shadow-black-background 635CSi badging is combined with the post-1987 spoiler and the chrome wraparound bumpers which were covered from Autumn 1987 onward in Europe.

Picture: David Shepherd, 1998

De-restricted in Nevada, these lucky M6 owners cut loose.

Picture: Klaus Schnitzer, September 1989

The Federal 633CSi was listed from 1978 and sold a strong 10,630 units, including just eight that left the showrooms tardily in 1986! Often the sole offering in the US 6-series store, this 1983 model typifies the 3.2-liter edition that sold a record 2,613 units in that year.

Picture: BMW NA, Otober 1983

Contrasting weather
and aluminum wheels,
but the same 1980s
633CSi product.
Sunshine or fog,
Federal bumpers
spoiled the lines of
even this classic
coupe.

Pictures: BMW North
America, undated and
February 1982

complete M-coupe weighed about 100 lb more than its simpler brethren, but the dramatic difference was in weight between European and American specifications.

For the M635 versus US M6 the figure was a daunting 245 lb, whereas for 12-valve 635s the gap was reported at 150 lb. In all cases I have used the average of independent test weights, not factory figures. My conclusion is that the negligible loss in torque for the US version (some 3.5 percent, compared to 12 percent horsepower drop across the Atlantic) was overlooked at the time and preserved more performance that we had a right expect in the US considering bhp losses and weight gains.

Chassis Finesse

Now, over to the transmission and chassis men to discover what they did. That is, aside from relocating the battery in the boot to counterbalance a front end weight bias measured at 55/45 percent in the UK and 52 versus 48 percent distribution in the US. Motorsport's competition chassis engineer Werner Frohwein, assisted by Herr Frings, finished up with an official 3300 lb (1500 kg) M-parcel to play with in Europe, carrying 53 percent over the front wheels and 47 percent over the rear.

An old but effective weight-relocation trick for the M-coupes was to displace the battery into the trunk.

Picture: BMW Werkfoto, 1983

Complete with the bodywork and running gear changes that we discuss later, the M635 was rated with a drag coefficient of 0.39 Cd with 53.3 inch height, and track figures of 56.3 inches front and 57.6 inches rear with the standard wheels and tires. What this meant was a vehicle substantially the same as 635 CSi in dimensions, plus 154 lbs (70 kg) official curb weight in Europe.

Aided by the translation efforts of Peter Locker, known to many of the BMW's sporting and subsequent BMW Individual customers, it was revealed that the technical problems for Motosport were really not the obstacle to redeveloping the M6 on the 635 base.

Company senior management caution over any new derivative was far more of a restriction than any technicality, for BMW Motorsport had been building and experimenting with various four valve combinations since 1977, when they had tried the 24-valve motor in the 5 Series. This merely fitted in with their usual exploratory moves of engine and model combination, and no official work on the M-Power 6 Series, outside the engine, was commercially undertaken before the eighties.

An M635 body was that of a Karmann-built 635 CSi with heavily massaged rear floorpan to accommodate the larger 7 Series final drive. Standard production ware inside that differential was a 25 percent ZF locking action, as optionally available on cheaper Sixes. Other important transmission moves were related to a completely new bellhousing that is integral with a Getrag 280/5 gearbox of five speeds, arranged in the traditional competition pattern with first isolated and closest to a left-hand driver.

Gear ratios were replaced: first was reported at 3.51; second, 2.08; third, 1.35; fourth a direct 1:1 and fifth an overdriven 0.81. The latter was asked to cooperate with a 3.73 final drive instead of 635's 3.07 and this yielded 23.87 mph per 1000 rpm. The revised gearing allowed 164.7 mph at the rpm limit of 6900 using 245 section Michelin TRXs on 16.3 inch unique TRX rims .

Drive was still taken up by a large single dry clutch plate, but the springs were considerably stronger. Even with the usual hydraulic leverage applied, you need a suitably sturdy left leg to control clutch action accurately and consistently.

The 2-door body had very modest wheelarch flares to accommodate some seriously wide rubber, tires that were originally European options. Standard for Europe in the mid-eighties were 220/55 Michelin TRX on 165 TR 390 (15.3 inch diameter) alloy wheels.

Then there was originally optional (standard in US) BBS three-piece alloy wheels of 210 TR 415 dimensions that accommodated radical 240/45 VR TRXs. The lowest and widest TRC alloy was replaced by the racy

Best of the best: M635CSi at launch on its sparkling alloys. BMW performance claims were for a 158 mph maximum and the run from 0–62 mph in 6.4 seconds.

Picture: BMW Werkfoto, 1983

BBS of 8.3 x 16.3 inches, the extra inch of diameter needed to compensate for that ultra low profile, as well as offering the best part of two inches extra rim width and an adhesive radial, nearly 9.5 inches wide. Some 1983 road car!

The suspension sounded straightforward with the usual BMW MacPherson strut front and the 13 degree angle of back trailing arms inherited from the 5 Series, but it was stunningly effective. Spring rates were stiffened "some 15 percent front and rear and about 10 mm removed from the ride height. We used the Bilstein gas dampers, specially developed for this car, and also went up on the (anti) roll bar thickness. At the back we use a progressive bar that gives an effect where only 0.5 mm increase gives an effective strength like you had added 2 mm," recalled Herr Frings in 1984.

The BMW engineer also added the information that a supplementary helper spring was installed within each front strut. " This is to counter the body roll you would otherwise get at the cornering speeds this M-car can go," he said with a small smile. One that spoke of treats to come, when we

Front discs grew to
11.8 inches (300 mm)
in diameter, 1.1 inches
(30 mm) thick, and sup-
ported anti-lock brakes
in all markets.

Picture: BMW Werkfoto,
1983

did get a pre-production chance to experience the most exhilarating BMW production 6 Series. We were not to be disappointed...

Brakes were naturally uprated, the emphasis being placed on front-end stopping power. Instead of 11 inches x 0.98 inches thick (280 mm x 25 mm) they installed cross-ventilated discs that measured a strapping 11.8 inches x 1.18 inches (300 mm x 30 mm) with 4-piston calipers drawn from ATE and the old M1-specification.

The discs were also grooved at the front, but at the back 11.2 inch (284 mm) vented units were fitted, braked with pistons having an extra 0.08inch (2 mm) circumference. The ABS anti-lock braking system had to be calibrated for the extra grip, weight and performance of the M635, ABS remaining a standard showroom item.

Ancillary cooling work for the engine transplant comprised a "larger and thicker" water radiator core and a thermostatically governed oil cooler. Remember, we are discussing a 24 valve engine that developed the peak 218 bhp of the traditional 12 valve 635 as a 4500 rpm preliminary to getting down to some serious business at higher revolutions!

A fabulous power unit in the BMW tradition, one that could spend much of its working life whooping to 6900 rpm and logging routine mileages in excess of 130,000 miles, all without major surgery.

Spring 1984, saw me visit the Dingolfing manufacturing plant, home to all 6 Series manufacture, appropriately driving a press fleet M635 CSi. Accompanied by present day Porsche PR Michael Schimpke in the boring two lane road trip north of Munich, I was relieved to find the tedious journey had been worthwhile. I am just so glad I was able to visit while the 6 Series was still running down the overhead tracks.

Back then, output of the M635 CSi was truly integrated with normal BMW output. The M-coupes were trickling along at about two a day, or about 500 a year, possibly because I timed my visit alongside a full scale metalworkers strike, a stoppage so unfamiliar, that I overheard my hosts wondering at this sudden visitation of the "English Disease!"

Looking through the M635/M6 statistics I can see that just three years surpassed output figures of 1000, 1984–5 and 1987; otherwise, production was measured in hundreds or 52 for the final (1989) year.

It was inspiring to watch the Six transform from bare metal shell to running automobile. A series of quality checks characterized the already

Spring 1984, and another 6 Series heads for the final badging ceremony at Dingolfing. Watching is then-BMW overseas press manager Michael Schimpke, who efficiently managed much of the unique access I enjoyed to research this book. Today, Schimpke is better-known at Porsche, but his taste for antiques of all kinds remains undimmed.

Picture: Republished from Author original of 1984

thorough progress checks made not only on 6 Series but also on the other BMW models seen steaming along the same overhead tracks. Finally it was anointed with the sacred Roundel and was ready for an extraordinarily thorough road test.

My main memory of that overcast day was of dodging the factory testers as they wheel-spun the M-coupes inside the plant, apparently just as unable to resist the temptation to gas the motor as the rest of us.

The M635/M6 was the ultimate expression of the 6 Series for showroom customers. Unfortunately for the racing BMW brotherhood, there was no way that the M for Motorsport badge could be used to redress 1984's increasing domination of the European Touring Car Championship by Jaguar, Volvo and Rover. It would be 1986 before BMW secured that European title again, and the 24-valve unit would not be part of that story.

BMW officials reiterated patiently that there was no way that engine manufacturing inside the Munich plant could cope with making 5000 of the 24-valve M6 power plants in a year. Prominent BMW 6 Series competitors such as Hans Stuck had originally hoped that the engine would be

Fancy being paid for this much fun! This Munich test driver is hard at work, "fine-tuning" the M-coupe's suspension.

Picture: BMW Archiv, 1998

With less than 6,000 manufactured, every one of the genuine M-coupes deserves a conscientious owner.

Picture: BMW Werkfoto, 1983

used to ease the power deficit of racing 3.4 liters against Jaguar's superb 5.3 liter V12 or Volvo's turbo terrors.

Now we will see how the 12 valve 635 was forced to defend BMW's reputation for racing the fleetest and fastest coupes to be found in European endurance racing.

QUICK FACTS

Product

Racing BMW 635 CSi coupe

Period

1980–86. From 1980-82 raced European Group 2, then World-wide Group A recognized 1 March 1983. Factory-backed : 1983-86

Production

E24 BMW 635CSi June 1978 to April 1989, total 45,213. More than 50 Group A BMW 635s were assembled and released by BMW Motorsport, most to non-factory teams

Performance

138 mph (road)/155 mph (race); 0-60 mph, 7.5 sec (road)/ 6.7 sec (race)

Achievements

Group A winners, 1983 (Dieter Quester) and 1986 (Roberto Ravaglia), European Championships. Jim Richards, 1985 Australian Champion in a Group A 635. 1981 European title (Group 2) and Group A Spa 24 hour races of 1983, 1985–86

People

Dieter Quester's last European title, 1983: Ravaglia's last-gasp 1986 Euro-title. Embryo Grand Prix stars Stefan Bellof and Gerhard Berger show F1 speed in coupes.

9 Racing 635:
Some You Win...

A showroom seductress, the 6 Series raced with honor across Europe and into Australia and New Zealand. Beneath the flowing lines was a heart tough enough to win the world's harshest sedan races

Replacing the racing CSL of the seventies by the 6 Series was not BMW's sporting intention when the later coupe line was announced. To mangle the old Jaguar advertising slogan, a 6 Series came with more grace and space, less pace than earlier coupes.

Racing was not a key development issue, yet the Sixer would outlast the 5.3 liter Jaguar V12s, Rover-Buick V8s and both Volvo and Ford turbos in the course of its unplanned race career.

The old "Batmobile" CSLs continued to race long after any factory "sell-by" date on either side of the Atlantic. Right through 1979, with barely a trace of factory backing and with their homologated right to race expiring at the close of the season, the obsolete (by three years) CSLs continued to race and win.

In 1979, the CSL won 12 of 13 European Championship rounds to score title gold in the last six of seven possible European Championship years. It was an impossible act to follow as other manufacturers queued to deprive BMW of their European Championship domination in the eighties, but still the 635 performed creditably.

Remember, the first Sixers carried more weight and had a larger frontal area to speed through the air. Also, 6 Series power trains—at least until the 24-valve motors came on stream in the mid-eighties—were not a significant advance over their predecessors. Such 24-valve units were not raced, because insufficient quantities were made within the 6 Series to pass the contemporary 5000 annual output requirement of International Group A.

Preliminary steps for racing the 6 Series were taken under the old FIA European Group 2 formula in 1980, requiring only a thousand produc-

The first of the Sixer's three European Championship titles came in 1981 from this radically modified 635CSi. Running to Group 2 specification, the Enny-backed coupe was a winner for Helmut Kelleners and Umberto Grano.

Picture: Courtesy Enny/ BMW, 1981

tion cars a year. This successful debut for the 635 was followed by the 1983 homologation in Group A of the 635CSi. Group A 635s grabbed most international success, but first we recall the Group 2 pioneer's record.

The first racing 635CSi for a European title hunt came from Racing Corporation Vienna. It was prepared to the tightened Group 2 regulations that had banned many of the trick items—four valve per cylinder heads, non-production gearboxes—of the earlier seventies Group 2 CSLs, and their rivals.

This early race 635 weighed in at 2618 lb (1190 kg), approximately 140 lbs (70 kg) heavier than the 24v CSLs of 1976. The previous racing BMW coupes also had almost 100 bhp more than the 367 bhp that the 12-valve six offered 1980 lead Group 2 635 driver Umberto Grano. The Italian's teammates were Austrians Herbie Werginz/Harald Neger and this trio won the opening two rounds of the 1980 European Championship, those of Monza and Vallelunga (also in Italy).

The pioneer race Six then had to concede best to the title-winning Egg-enberger BMW 320i of that year, winning only one more race, albeit the prestigious British Tourist Trophy round at Silverstone. From September

1980, BMW Italia became more seriously involved in the European Championship and backed a second 635CSi, whose drivers included double Belgian Spa 24 hour winner (in a 530i US) Eddy Joosen.

During 1981, the 635 again appeared in Group 2 format for Europe, this time with more overt BMW support and Enny leather goods sponsorship. Drivers were Grano and German veteran Helmut Kelleners. They wrapped up a series that became more competitive with the advent of the new Group A regulations for 1982.

BMW met the 1982 European challenge of a Jaguar V12 XJ-S prepared by TWR and backed by Motul, this becoming a brace of Jaguars from mid-season onward. By 1983, Volvo 240 turbos, TWR Rover SD1 V8s (running an alloy construction V8 descended from a sixties Buick or Oldsmobile), all wanted to come and beat previously "unbeatable" BMW and those TWR Jaguars. These Jags became official works entries, coated in British racing green as of 1983.

The European race pace heated up, but BMW was ill-equipped for the rule-bending that inevitably followed. BMW Motorsport was forced to field the less powerful 528i for 1982, while the 635CSi was not homolo-

The most famous Group A racing colors for 635CSi, and a fitting fourth championship winner for Dieter Quester. Here is the *Original Teile* (Original Parts) Schnitzer coupe for Quester in that Championship year of 1983. The big coupe would win a final title, this time for Roberto Ravaglia, in 1986.

Those 1980s titles were fantastic achievements as the opposition was the heaviest that BMW had ever faced in the European title hunt. It included V12 Jaguars, turbocharged Volvos and Fords, and Rover V8 sedans. And the luxurious 635 was never intended to be a racer!

Picture: BMW Archiv, 1998/Taken from a 1983 original

Thirty years a winning BMW driver! This must be a record among racers, but here is proof: Dieter Quester is in top form at Aspern, Vienna, Austria in 1966 with the 1800 "Tisa" (top). Then we see him out at practice work in the 635 during 1986 (bottom). Quester went on to race M3s regularly and even raced (and won outright) in the 1800 "Tisa" again for Scuderia Bavaria in the 1990s.

For the 1996 Monterey Historic events, Quester was reunited with one of several Group A 625s that BMW Mobile Tradition keeps in 1990s running order.

Pictures: BMW Werkfotos, 1986

gated for Group A until 1 March 1983. As stated, a 24-valve M5 and M6 motor never made it to Group A race recognition, owing to strict German ONS sporting authority inspection procedures, as well as restricted manufacturing numbers.

Having homologated and modestly supported the 2.8 liter 5 Series, BMW knew they needed more cubic capacity to meet the V12 Jaguar and turbocharged models from Volvo (a 240 variant), Ford (initially the Merkur XR4Ti) and Mitsubishi (Starion coupe).

The 635 CSi was the only sporting BMW variant produced in sufficient numbers with the company's then-largest production power plant to qualify for 5000 per annum Group A. Thus a 12-valve single cam six became mandatory over the obviously more potent DOHC 24-valve unit.

There were to be no dramatic homologation moves from BMW on the 635CSi, and the coupe was regularly outpaced, especially in practice sessions over one banzai lap. Yet the 635 turned out to be the glamorous workhorse of European Championship racing.

Good enough to secure Dieter Quester another Euro title (1983). Strong enough to dominate the first six places in the last Nürburgring 6 hours to be held, also in 1983. That season the 635 also established the first of three victories at Spa, Europe's most prestigious 24 hour race for sedans.

Race 635 CSi hardware

Depending on formula, team funds and race length, the specification of any racing 6 Series proved pretty flexible. At the heart of the best results would be a pile of factory supplied parts, varying from reinforced bare body to the electronics required for racing, plus big brakes and replacement suspension components.

Purely as a test car, I was fortunate enough to drive a 1983 factory-supplied and assisted Group A 635 CSi in Britain, the machine normally driven by Hans Joachim Stuck that season. I have taken what I learned at that time, and in the 1982/83 winter purchased a racing 635 kit from Munich that became the Grace International CSi for Frank Sytner (one of Britain's biggest BMW and Alpina dealers), to guide us through what went into the racing preparation of an early eighties Group A 635.

First, a few factory facts from the production line, for they were relevant to the racer. The competition coupe was comparatively lowly tuned, but used a large number of proven race-only replacement components in the transmission and suspension.

It was factory production changes that assisted a low race curb weight 2554 lb (1161 kg), so that 635 had to be ballasted to reach the class minimum of 2607 lb (1185 kg). Remember, the production 6 Series had gone through substantial early eighties alterations, including a chop in curb weight of more than 132 lb (60 kg). It had also adopted 7 Series double link front suspension and 5 Series based rear trailing arms (13 degree trailing angles).

There were no lightweight panel tricks, but BMW was not initially able to get the FIA to recognize the showroom use of plastics for the front spoiler and rain gutters, plus the rubber material of the back spoiler. These items had to join the Group A specification retrospectively.

BMW had anticipated the worst in crash test regulations during the Sixer's production gestation, and the early Group 2 racers had to live with that bulk. Once in production, BMW found that they could provide at least the same crash test performance without the designated heavy duty steel grades or body construction. Weight was shaved back in the summer of 1982, and it was in this format that the 635 did its factory supported Group A miles.

For the street, a 635 was rated at 218 bhp by 5200 rpm and 224 lb-ft of torque on 4000 rpm. Compression escalated from 9.3:1 to 10:1 in the summer 1982 change over to 3430 cc and reflected more sophisticated Bosch Digital Motor Electronics (DME).

For Group A competition the 3430cc six was selected, but with a standard 86mm crankshaft throw and maximum homologation tolerance allowing a bore of 92.6 mm instead of a production 92 mm, the SOHC six reached 3475.07 cc. The 7-bearing steel crankshaft with 12 counterweights retained its production sources, steel connecting rods supporting cast aluminum Mahle race pistons, which operated an 11.1 compression.

In race terms, the most radical engine design was applied to the 324 degree camshaft timing and lift, supporting 46 mm inlet and 38 mm exhaust valve head sizes. The cylinder head intake porting was reworked and smoothed to flow extra incoming mixture, blended to the inlet manifolding.

These handcrafted moves were allied to reprogrammed Bosch Motronic to govern ignition and injection. If I sound vague about the precise moves made I can only quote what Alpina boss Burkard Bovensiepen said to me in the spring of 1984, " We have nothing written down about these engines, because with Group A you just must not write about such things!"

Inside and out, the 635CSi adapted to racing extremely well, although the amount of interior trim demanded by the authorities for Group A looked odd alongside a light-weight racing seat and steering wheel. The race weight was 2,607 lbs (1,185 kg). and horsepower was declared at 285 bhp. Behind the white-topped 5-speed manual shifter are rows of easy-access fuses and circuit breakers, plus the master ignition switch and button starter.

The lower phantom view reveals the engine-bay brace and center-lock, quick-release BBS multi-spoke race wheels.

Pictures: BMW Werkfoto, 1984

This is Alpina's version of the Group A racing 635 single-camshaft motor. In a coupe driven extensively by Hans Stuck in Britain, it delivered 285 bhp at 6,000 rpm and 257 lb-ft of torque by 5,000 rpm. Theoretically, it was not enough to get the job done, but BMW beat a lot of cars with more power and less weight through reliability, Schnitzer racecraft, and amazing durability under attack from some of the world's hardest drivers.

Picture: LAT, 1983

Official power and torque for an Alpina-BMW Group A 3.5 liter in 1983 was quoted at 285 bhp by 6000 rpm, with 257 lb-ft of torque at 5000 rpm. That meant its maximum power bonus was delivered 800 rpm up on a street coupe, while peak torque moved 1000 rpm up the scale, very mild figures by international motor racing standards and allowing phenomenal 24 hour racing durability.

The 12-valve track car had power capabilities similar to a street 24-valve M635 in a lot less curb weight. The race 635 was 539 lbs (245 kg) less than the curb weight of a street 635CSi.

One of 25 Alpina-BMW 3.5 liter race engines delivered by spring 1984 revealed the extraction of an extra 67 bhp and 29 lb-ft of bonus torque under Group A rules, but it had Burkard Bovensiepen sighing, "Much of the work is the electronics from Bosch, and this is so expensive for the private tuner or owner. Bosch [doesn't] want people re-programming their electronics and the prices are too high for customers ."

This electronic programming era, and German racing sedans that became progressively more race and less sedan, did not suit Alpina policy of supplying parts to privateers. Alpina's race star began to lose its twinkle during the mid-eighties. Schnitzer, who franchised their public sale performance conversions and parts supplies out under a licensing agreement branded AC Schnitzer, became correspondingly stronger, especially in the light of their European and Spa 24 hours campaigns of the factory-supplied 635CSi racing coupes.

The Stuck car in 1983 was pretty typical of how the 635 stayed in touring car trim for 1983–86, for the restrictive Group A regulations strangled normally aspirated motors. Even if you flowed more mixture to the combustion chambers, there was the problem of extracting burnt gases, for the cast iron manifolding had to remain that of production vehicles. Also, both valve lift and size was regulated.

Such constrictions, plus German officialdom and their understandable reluctance to falsify production figures, meant the 635CSi stayed right around 285 bhp through the racing mid-eighties. That gave a power to weight ratio of 243.6 bhp a ton, better than racing 528i, but no match for a V12 Jaguar or a turbocharged Volvo.

In action BMW's 285 bhp would speed the 635 to 150 mph, but this was not in the same league as the rapidly developing Jaguar V12s. These TWR coupes developed 420 bhp and 440 lb-ft of torque and could rev to 7000 rpm by 1984. That meant fifth gear would see the Big Cats in the 165 mph bracket on any decent straightaway.

The 635 was surprisingly manageable on a race track, particularly compared to the Jaguar. Respective racing weights of 2607 lb (1185 kg) for the race 635 and 3080 lb (1400 kg) for the Jaguar underlined the reasons for this comparative BMW agility in a near 16 foot long 2-door.

There were three choices of final drive ratio from 3.07 to 3.91:1, and a ZF limited slip differential usually set at 75 percent pre-load. The big gearbox definitely had CSL heritage and the Getrag provided the same good natured synchromesh command of four ratios in an H-pattern, first then isolated on a dogleg, closest to the left-hand driver.

Gear ratios were radically different with a 2.33 first gear as compared to a 3.822 on the wide ratio stock gearbox, and the racer had appropriately close ratios thereafter. This allowed a suitably "tall" first for racing getaways, most of which were rolling start affairs in Europe. In Britain and Australia, they stuck with standing starts for their national race series, and the standard single disc plate would wilt under that 6000 rpm strain.

BMW Motorsport specified the sweet-shifting Getrag 5-speed with the following ratios (1986 US showroom 5-speed in brackets) for most race tasks: first 2.33 (3.83); second, 1.68 (2.20); third, 1.353 (1.40); fourth 1.146 (1:1 direct); fifth a direct 1:1. A US 635CSi for 1986 had the usual street provision of an overdriven top gear (0.81) to save precious gas.

There were massive replacement brake sizes quoted on the March 1, 1983 racing Group A homologation (FIA #A-5118) and either Ate in Germany or AP Racing in Britain would supply components. The biggest competition-homologated front brake size was 13.1 inches (332 mm) and that was matched by a 12.4 inch (315 mm) rear, both 21.1 inch (8 mm) thick and clamped by the beefiest in light alloy calipers with 4-piston operation. The balance of braking effort, front to rear, was controlled by a cockpit-adjustable turn-wheel.

For comparison, note that the contemporary 1983 model 635 was recognized in the showroom with cast iron brake discs of 282 and 284 mm diameters (around 11.2 inches, some two inches less than the racing derivative), just 25 (front) and 10 mm thick. Unlike the race cars, a showroom 635 had standard ABS braking and hydraulic servo assistance.

The rest of a racing 635 undercarriage was beautifully crafted and proven in the toughest of higher power situations. The suspension had to act on the same principles as those found in production, but many replacement components carried over from the Group 2/IMSA CSL coupes of the seventies, via the 1982 Group A racing 528 to 635.

Initial test runs of 3.5 liter 635 race power train were perfomed in a converted Group A 528i, including suspension and brakes. These interchangeable items covered some of the big brake/wheel bearing options and fabricated suspension components, including sturdily reinforced rear suspension arms with box-sections.

For 1983 BMW Motorsport offered replacement lower arms for the front MacPherson struts, replacement rear trailing arms, solid joints for key suspension components, replacement rear differential bushes, center lock wheel nuts and a selection of three Bilstein spring/damper choices that multiplied as the seasons rolled by.

Wheels and tires were BBS multi-piece 11 x 16 inch alloys in 1983. It was shod by Dunlop in the UK, but Pirelli was the favored supplier for the most successful Schnitzer BMW 635s of mid-1984 onward.

I tested the 1983 Group A 635 on 1200 lb/inch front springs and 750 lb/in rears, but the British demands were at odds with Europe for increasing spring stiffness and stiffer anti-roll bars. That Donington circuit test car had 32 mm/1.25 inch front and 20 mm/0.8 inch rear anti-roll bars. Generally, Sixers built for longer distance European events were set softer, absorbed bumps better, but were not so agile through increased body lean that was most evident on sharper, slower, curves.

The steering remained on the ball and nut steering box system, but you could opt for either the standard 14.5:1 or a quicker 13.6:1 ratio. Power assistance was deleted for shorter events, but many of the longer distance

It says Hans Stuck on the side, but the author was lucky enough experience some sunny laps in the factory-supported racer supplied in 1983 to defend BMW's honor in Britain. Stuck was on hand for another routine test day, but for me, it was a memorable outing that punched home just what a fine race coupe the 635 became.

Picture: LAT/*Motoring News*, 1983

Schnitzer coupes—especially those driven by Hans Stuck—did use power assisted steering to cut driver fatigue.

Teutonic attention to detail extended to the interior of a body that required additional body seam welding before competing. The standard dashboard molding remained and the 42 lb (19 kg) aluminum Rubi roll cage was spanner-adjustable to take in any slop that developed in the racing body over thousands of competition kilometers.

BMW could also supply all the electronic wiring loom, a three spoke (flat with padded center: such luxury!) steering wheel, 7-dial VDO instrumentation, Recaro racing seat and Autoflug 6-point race harness. Competition 635s all came in LHD from the factory, but BMW GB supported a brace of 1984 coupes that did have British/Japanese right drive steering.

Nobody pretended that the Group A racing 635 was a stock showroom item and it was an expensive proposition, being hand built (often at German labor rates) from the stronger bare body outward. From the factory viewpoint it still had a stock 635 outline. From the driver's seat it was exceptionally friendly to drive. Here I am not thinking just of my own dry road test experience, but also of now US-based motorsports journalist Jeremy Shaw's outing in the pouring wet of a Silverstone race with a Hartge 635CSi.

Only when Shaw had finished his final 40-lap stint in the prestigious Tourist Trophy did he find that the pit crew had left slick racing tires for dry road use on one side of the vehicle... and treaded wet weather covers on the other side! Few other such powerful rear drive cars were so well-mannered in 1984.

The near 540 lb weight reduction over stock, plus the wide power curve of the 285 bhp motor was independently tested by Germany's *auto motor und sport* (*ams*) magazine. Built for rolling starts with that long racing ratio first gear, *ams* discovered 0–60 mph in 6.9 sec, 0–96 mph in 13.6 sec; 0–124 mph occupied 23.6 sec and the quarter mile around 14.5 seconds.

The factory gave the maximum speed as 155 mph on the tallest ratio and the longest straight. I was privileged to also test drive the TWR XJ-S and would say the 635 was at least 15 mph down on the 165 mph Jaguar V12 in most racing situations. It was certainly outgunned by the 330-360 turbo horsepower of the brick-like Volvos.

A compensation was the comparatively frugal race day fuel consumption, equating to between 5.7 and 5.9 (6.9 and 7.1 UK mpg). This allowed the 635 to gain vital track time over the more frequent pit stops of its more powerful rivals.

Left-hand-drive was retained for the British-domiciled racing 635. The helmeted author sits in the cabin, talking to racing preparation specialist Bob Sparshott about the world's most comfortable competition coupe. This UK example is one of more than 50 supplied by the factory to racing teams around the globe.

Picture: LAT, 1983

"This is how our competitors should see the 'Genuine Parts' BMW coupe," said BMW's press office of this 1984 shot of Dieter Quester in action at Monza, Italy.

Picture: BMW Werkfoto, 1984

The Group A track record

The 635BMW represented a Schnitzer turning point in Freilassing's working relationship with BMW in Munich. Charly Lamm's Schnitzer team management was unmatched for European endurance racing strategy.

Mix Lamm's intellect, Schnitzer pit-work under the management of Herbert Schnitzer (founder engineer and championship-winning driver Josef Schnitzer died in 1978) and BMW's fabled long distance speed—now you have the recipe for BMW to become the most successful sedan endurance racers around the World. The 635 nobly enhanced that legendary reputation during four factory backed seasons, 1983–86.

What results did the racing 6 Series achieve in Group A trim? Underlining 635's fortitude in allweather racing were its long distance performances, for the fabulous Six won a trio of Spa 24 hour races between 1983–86, and only stopped winning when factory backing switched to the M3.

This achievement was only overshadowed by BMW's unequaled company record since 1964 in the Belgian 24 hour classic. The Bavarians have now scored 20 outright wins in 34 editions of the Ardennes day and night grind, compared to six victories from Ford, four for Porsche and single wins accorded to Jaguar, Mazda, Nissan and Mercedes.

In 1983 BMW set the 635 the task of maintaining its fortunes at Spa. True, they had won in 1982 with the 528 (crushing any opposition with a one thru six finishing order!) but had suffered a comparatively long drought as Ford took a hat trick of Capri V6 victories from 1978-80. Then TWR pushed the rotary Mazda RX-7 to noisy victory in 1981.

BMW backed its big coupes in what was to become their most famous livery (Genuine Parts/Original Teile) and the M Technic branding. Although the Sixers were prepared to similar mechanical specifications, they were run by the Belgian Juma tuning/official importer organization, as well as the higher profile Schnitzer connection.

Perhaps an even more telling testimony to BMW's reputation and the racing efficiency of the 635CSi was that 17 such cars were entered in 1983. Many privateers obviously trusted BMW's reputation to get them to the finish in a then new racing version of the coupe.

That trust was rewarded. Some 11 of that 17-strong confidence vote finished inside the top twenty in an event notable for a BMW 635CSi placing a 1-2 win. In 1983 Schnitzer were new boys on the Spa block. Juma (headed by Julien Mampaey) was the establishment when it came to preparing Spa-winning BMWs and it was a Juma-prepared 635CSi that won for drivers Thierry Tassin, Armin Hahne and Hans Heyer.

However, Schnitzer were second for drivers Winkelhock, Quester and Rossi. The Freilassing equip from the Austro-German southern border countryside would become the most successful BMW preparation/ pit-work team to date.

The 1983–97 Formula 1 ace Gerhard Berger followed his Austrian countryman Niki Lauda in racing a BMW sedan from 1984 onward. That first outing brought neither BMW nor Berger a win, for 1984 was the first and last time to date that Jaguar won Belgium's 24 hours. The Jags were a magnificent sight and sound as their TWR twelves echoed amongst the tall pines, remorselessly pursued by a flotilla of Munich's finest sonorous Sixes.

Subsequent Grand Prix winner Gerhard shared a winning 635 in the 1985 Spa 24 hours, and the second car home that year was a 635, too. In 1985, Berger set fastest lap, in excess of 96 mph over Spa's purpose-built (in 1979) Ardennes curves. There were six BMWs in the top ten finishers, versus a brace of Volvos and Alfa GTV6s.

In 1986, the 635 proved the 24 hour point comprehensively, the big Bimmers monopolizing the front four places, BMW also home fifth with a gallant little 325i. But Italian star Roberto Ravaglia was not the winner, as you would have expected from his winning ways of 1986. What happened to Ravaglia and the leading 635CSi he shared with Berger and Emanuele Pirro?

It was a leading runner. Unlike the BMW 635 that would win for Dieter Quester/Altfrid Heger and the injured Thierry Tassin, it also avoided the sand traps, or any subsequent need for an illicit tow! Ravaglia and company were leading until 2 hours 15 minutes prior to the 5 p.m. finish.

Then an alternator bracket cruelly fractured and its Schnitzer-BMW team mate (both in the famous white BMW Parts livery) thundered through to win. The result was the BMW 635 haul of the first four finishing positions, fifth taken by BMW as well, for the Voigt 325i defeated a French-prepared Mercedes 190.

In hindsight the best year for non-24 hour race results and the BMW 635 was the first, 1983. Then the turbo cars were not so well-muscled as they would become, and their reliability was suspect. Bigger capacity Jags and Rovers were then not always durable enough for the sweaty and lengthier slogs around Europe, either.

Just at the start of a Grand Prix career that would take in winning ways at McLaren and Ferrari, Austria's Gerhard Berger was probably the fastest of a very fleet driver squad employed regularly by BMW to compete in the factory-backed Schnitzer 635s. Here he is, part of the winning team at Spa in 1985.

Picture: Heide Nicot for BMW AG, 1985

BMW won the first 1983 European Championship encounter—held at Monza in March a decade after the lightweight CSL debuted—against Jaguar. BMW filled eight of the top ten spots after 310.5 miles (500 kms) of the legendary Italian track.

After a season full of incident as TWR sorted the Jaguars into winning propositions, I went along to see the final European Championship round. On September 25 1983, Zolder in Belgium was the badly-organized venue.

The season could not have been closer since both BMW and Jaguar had won five European Championship rounds apiece, the only other qualifier going to TWR Rover V8s. The front runners—16 of them—practiced within 2.5 sec of each other and there were 46 runners and riders to watch.

Stefan Bellof hit the front for BMW and led much of the opening 35 laps, but nothing could take that much abuse and last an hour, never mind a slog from sunshine into twilight. The other BMWs did last the pace and supported Dieter Quester as his Schnitzer coupe scooped up another Championship. It was BMW's 13th title in the 17 years since they had contested the European Championship, for Hubert Hahne won their first European Drivers title back in 1966.

This was Quester's fourth and last European title, but BMW won again with the 635 in 1986 and took two more titles with the original M3, before the European series folded in 1988.

Today, BMW continues to contest some events that were part of that European series—their record in the annual Spa 24 hours apparently strengthening by the year. Nobody offers BMW serious opposition at home on the old Nürburgring—but today the international accent is on shorter national 2-liter SuperTourer events, a category that is no automatic BMW domain in the later nineties.

The 1983 story in Britain was of much promise but no championship results. The Hans Stuck/Cheylesmore Alpina-engined 635 never managed to best the Rover V8s on track, even though the TWR Rovers were subsequently disqualified.

Stuck versus Steve Soper, in the TWR Rover in Hepolite Pistons colors, delivered some epic race spectating in the UK.

I remember that yellow Rover and its able graduate driver, particularly as it had been an objective of my 1982 winter trip to BMW Motorsport (accompanying racing team technician and owner Ted Grace and Malcolm Gartlan) to persuade BMW that Steve Soper was the right choice as a British-based works BMW driver in a 635 for 1983.

Now the proprietor of a major motor-trade chain, Frank Sytner also drove the 635 and M3 with distinction, winning Britain's premier sedan championship with the M3 prepared by Prodrive. Here is a shot from the 1984 season, when most media attention was concentrated on the ultimately successful fight by the British authorities to have the TWR Rovers disqualified from their apparent 1983 British title win.

Picture: LAT/*Motoring News*, 1984

BMW's contemporary sports manager, Dieter Stappert, was willing to listen. Motorsport did let us buy a racing package to assemble in the UK, but Steve Soper was retained inside the Rover Group for several more seasons. Steve went on winning for Rover and Ford before finally joining BMW in 1989. He was still contracted as one of four star drivers by the Munich company in 1998.

In 1984, Europe TWR returned with a trio of the V12-powered Jaguar XJ-S coupes in British Racing Green and factory livery. BMW wins became scattered, only Helmut Kelleners and Gianfranco Brancatelli offering consistent opposition. A Belgian BMW Team entry for France's Danny Snobeck/Alain Cudini did win an early event—despite a freak accident that involved another BMW mounting their coupe!

The only other 1984 compensation was that Volvo had enough pace to win, so it was not Jaguar all the time...it just seemed like it. At home in Germany, the press gave BMW a roasting. Then national German media turned to the preparation of the winning Jaguars. German magazine market leader *auto motor und sport* asserted British illegality, and illustrated their complaints, particularly in regard to fuel carried and engine size: both were alleged oversized.

Nothing was proven, and the combination of Tom Walkinshaw and the Jaguars his company prepared took the 1984 European title. In contrast, TWR's unstoppable run of wins in the 1983 British series was successfully protested by BMW dealer/driver Frank Sytner. TWR Rovers contesting the British title were retrospectively disqualified halfway into 1984, fines and costs totaling £100,000 imposed by the RAC national sporting authority.

BMW finished 1984 with just three European wins. Spa offered no compensation as that was Jaguar's 1984 triumph in a year when the Coventry cats with Oxfordshire preparation from TWR netted the European title.

BMW would not win the European title in 1985, but BMW gained compensation from an unusual source. Former Ford-contracted sedan champion Frank Gardner had returned to Australia and assembled some immaculate JPS-liveried (John Player Special, a cigarette brand) BMWs.

In 1985, expatriate New Zealander Jim Richards demonstrated his smoother driving skills at the wheel of a shimmering black and gold Bimmer to beat Mustangs with some 120 bhp extra to the title of Australian Touring Car Champion. Richards was not content to just sit and pick up points either, winning the penultimate Australian round in style, even though just a twelfth place was required.

On his winning season with the Pirelli-shod 635, Richards reflected laconically, "It's a beaut thing to drive. The harder you drive it, the faster it goes."

For Europe in 1985, Volvo did get their turbocharged act together and 350 bhp Swedish box-cars became regular winners, securing the European title for Brancatelli. Highspot of the BMW racing year was the victory of Gerhard Berger, Marc Surer and Roberto "Bob Ravioli" Ravaglia over its sister Schnitzer coupe at Spa 24 hours, but BMW struggled for race qualifying pace.

A brace of Eggenberger Volvo turbos surprised most to manage third and fourth on much reduced boost. Even the long distance challenge of Spa saw the 1985 Volvo race winning threat as real as it became in 1996 English and Australian 2-liter events. Incidentally, those nineties race 850/S40 Volvos were created by TWR, while other divisions of Tom Walkinshaw's nineties' empire (now with over 1200 employees worldwide!) raced Nissan at Le Mans, Yamaha motors in 1997 Grand Prix and Holden for Australian 5 liter V8 rules.

The rest of 1985 was pretty unhappy for von BimmerHeads. Best BMW championship points tally at the end went to Ravaglia, ninth in the over 2500 cc class behind a horde of Volvos and Rovers. Some you lose...

It was the worst result I can recall researching for BMW in the European sedan series. Schnitzer did not contest all the Championship rounds, while Berger put in some fabulous work at the wheel of the outclassed 635 on their combined appearances.

Yet 1986 was the season BMW won the overall driver's title again—Ravaglia and his Schnitzer-entered works 635CSi initially missed out by just one point to Briton Win Percy (Rover V8), and the contest went right down to the final wire. Immediate compensation came from a BMW 325i winning its division and completing the top three, overall.

As you would expect, "Bob Ravioli" was always in the top three podium pace throughout the 1986 season. During 1986, Roberto Ravaglia starred in four first place finishes for the Schnitzer equip in Europe. Roberto took the '86 fight for the Euro title to the last Portuguese round at the Estoril GP track.

Others did the physical stuff: Dieter Quester even rammed an Australian Holden (GM product) V8 in an effort to improve Ravaglia's finishing position versus the Rover of Win Percy!

However, Roberto ended the race, and the season, with 218 points accrued to the winning 219 total of the Briton and his eight cylinder TWR Rover. BMW could be proud of Roberto's ambassadorial diplomacy, for he smiled and said, "There's always next year."

Splintered spoilers and battered fronts made no difference: the big Bimmers went on winning right up to the end of their racing lives, replaced only by the purpose-built M3.

Picture: BMW Archiv, 1998/From a 1986 original

Photo finish. The
Schnitzer BMWs that
won the Spa 24-hours
of 1986, also placing
third, cross the down-
hill start-and-finish line
on Sunday afternoon.
Overall victory went to
the No. 11 car (with
split front spoiler, proof
of a rugged outing) for
Dieter Quester, Thierry
Tassin, and Altfrid
Heger. The third-placed
BMW was crewed by
Roberto Ravaglia,
Emanuele Pirro, and
Gerhard Berger.

Picture: BMW Werkfoto,
1986

Yet Roberto Ravaglia was finally declared the official champion by the
FIA officials in Paris at the close of 1986 play. It was this sort of reversal of
on-track race results that weakened the credibility of the European series
to the point where it was dropped at the end of 1988.

Ravaglia progressed to become BMW's most successful driver, winning
most European-centered Championships; the Venetian BMW dealer gathered up World, European, Italian and German titles for BMW before his
retirement at the close of 1997.

During the 1986–87 winter BMW Motorsport was intensively developing the M3 and there was the possibility that the 3.5 liter 635CSi might
prove quicker than its 2.3 liter junior, so much so that the thought of running the 635 CSi on into the opening three races of 1987 was made public.

Back-to-back BMW Motorsport/Schnitzer trials were conclusive: the
M3 was up to two seconds a lap quicker, even when it was far from its predicted 300 bhp.

The sensational showroom coupe that BMW never intended to race
could be pensioned off, complete with a race and championship pedigree
that many purpose-built competitions cars do not equal.

QUICK FACTS

Product

All 6 Series, purchase information;
850 production comment

Period

1989–98

Performance

From $6600 trailer-potato to $12,000
front line business coupe. Hear how
the author blew future residuals at the
body shop, stalled out on the first drive
and then entered the Promised Land

People

Knowledge shared, from the World
biggest BMW Club, through the Internet
and personal experience

10 Tips for Today

Living with 6 Series today, and why the 8 Series never made it to the BMW Hall of Fame

Sometimes it is not so easy being a big BMW fan. Rarely does the company foist a product on the public that the committed follower can not feel some sort of appreciation for. On May 16, 1990, a meltdown May day, I arrived in Munich and drove for a couple of days in examples of the first BMWs I instinctively disliked... their first coupe that failed to become a must-have.

Then simply called 850i, BMW's replacement for the 6 Series was on display at the Frankfurt Show in September 1989, some five months after the last of 86,216 Sixes had fled the lines at Dingolfing. The 850i was the second BMW—indeed the second postwar German car of any make—to carry V12 power, the first having been the 750i sedan.

The newcomer had some super technical tricks, including a manual 6-speed gearbox, a convoluted, heavy and efficient rear axle layout and an aerodynamic drag factor slashed below 0.30 Cd. In fact you could say the original 850 had too much of everything for public taste, for the 300 bhp machine in the near 4000 lb sharp suit sold under 30,000 copies in six full production years and was being made at the rate of less than 1500 a year in the last season for which we have figures; the last full year for 6 Series saw 3666 made.

Like better BMWs, the 850 was developed to take a number of alternative engines, and these made a much better sports coupe of it, but never a race track possibility; it was much too fat for that. BMW first tried putting the smallest V8 in the front bay, but the 1992 pre-production of 13 automatics and five manual transmission 830i coupes convinced them that the heavy 8 Series was never going to sparkle in that format.

For 1993, Munich made a much more popular move, inserting the 4-litre V8 and going on to manufacture 5598 of these in the next three years, outselling the V12 original from 1994 onward. It was withdrawn from UK sale post-1996. However, BMW had by then made an earth-shattering 850CSi which drew on Motorsport division's expertise to wake up the V12 in 5.6 liter/340 bhp trim—nothing like the lightweight 48-valve monster they had planned as M8, but one mighty coupe, and one that restored some sheer driving pleasure to the big BMW coupe sector.

Unfortunately the more expensive 5.6 liter 8 Series was just what the public did not want in volume, so sales figures were modest, some 1530 made from 1992–96. The original 850i was not made after August 1994, but an 850Ci derivative continued the V12 coupe line until 1995.

850 statistics versus 6 Series

I have only 1989–96 official statistics for the 8 Series—that means 840 V8 and 850 V12s; an 830 was pre-produced to the tune of 18 copies in 1992, but never made mass production.

Such figures show that BMW very nearly made the 850 their most popular big coupe of all time in 1991, making 9505 examples. Unfortunately

The author went to the 850i debut drive sessions in Munich, prepared to be overawed. Drove three or four examples over two days. Listened to the technical arguments from then-technical supremo Wolfgang Reitzle. Returned unimpressed. Remained so until the 5.6 liter 850CSi, which provided a truly involving drive, but by then sales had slumped. Perhaps a case of too much, too late?

Picture: BMW Werkfoto, 1989

Munich's masterwork to replace the 6 Series was slightly flawed and sold less than 30,000 units in six production years, as compared to more than 86,200 units for the 6 Series in nine years.

Picture: BMW Werkfoto, 1989

for BMW, the 6 Series of 1985 hit 9626 copies and had a far more consistent output, year on year. From 1989 to 1996 BMW manufactured just 28,292 of all 850/840 types and output plummeted after 1991. Most years saw production in the 2000 band (3095 for 1993) and well under the 2000 mark at just 1465 of 850Ci/840i manufactured during 1996.

BMW had failed to replace both the Six and its legendary coupe forebears in the public's affections with the 8 Series. If press-time speculation was correct, you will find that the 6 Series badge will become BMW's prestige coupe again in the Millennium. So our story probably has yet another chapter or two to be written!

Buying in the US

Just as in Britain, buying any Sixer in the US is normally a deal done between two consenting adults, miles from any official BMW dealership. That means the inspection of any potential purchase effectively becomes your guaran-

Weather bad, body good. Author's 635 after front fender replacement, before the Amtrak van struck.

Picture: Author, January 1998

tee—it's up to you to assess condition and likely upcoming repair costs. Even if you are going to a BMW specialist, or more especially if you see a Sixer on a lot with a lot of non-BMWs, take a knowledgeable friend along.

You may be an ace mechanic, but that third party could spot ownership documents that are not kosher, chassis/engine numbers which don't tally or homemade service stamps. Try to see a minimum of three and preferably six similar Sixers before buying, so that you know what you are looking for, and that the intended car feels right for your circumstances.

Here are the key considerations that the English climate (similar to New England, but with less snow) taught me, along with American viewing and the generous Web knowledge supplied by BMW CCA members the leading specialists in the States. Specialist addresses can be found on the page for this book on the publisher's web site (see the copyright page at the beginning of this book for the address), and are only given where it is obvious that members are satisfied with the services provided. Even if you don't have a BMW in the family right now, I would still start by joining the BMW Car Club of America (BMW CCA). Subscription was $35 annual when this was written, for which you got possibly the best club car magazine in the world along with a healthy sprinkling of 6 Series for sale in the classified sections. Try to attend at least two or three club gatherings, preferably two regional and one national, because you will be taught plenty in double quick time by a membership that has always appeared friendly and informative even to a visiting Limey.

What to check?

Start off by walking slowly around the car. Is it consistent with the way it has been described? Assuming you are not buying a wreck or a known trailer car, do the panels fit along regular shut lines? Do the doors, hood and trunk operate without groans? Watch out for the hood to stay propped upright on its gas struts—they often weaken with age and fall on inquisitive motor bay heads!

Step back a pace or two. Are the wheels and tires free from obvious curbing and associated sidewall damage? Is this a car that has been driven with respect, free of all but those everyday parking dings? Look under the back bumper to see any damage which may be poorly repaired. Most

The side stripes are not original, nor is that late model rear spoiler, but handsome "Helga" still warms the author's heart on a cold winter day.

Picture: Author, January 1998

cheap repairs concentrate on the shiny stuff and ignore the mangled panels below. I know, I saw many exactly like that!

The shinier it is, the harder you will find it to say "no", but be aware that some of the worst underbelly problems come with the shiniest exteriors. That is why you look for a consistency in the car's appearance with evidence of regular servicing. Expect to see the first 20–50,000 miles and one to four years stamped at an official dealership, followed by non-franchised care. If the car is older, and the owner does the work himself, look for regular maintenance item bills in support of that labor.

With every panel (including the sunroof) open, start checking for rust. If the Sixer lives in Arizona or Nevada, lucky you. Stop looking smug and double your inspection of any possible accident repair damage.

In damper climates, expect to see some rust around the front strut towers, and in both front and rear wheel arch seams. Just make sure that it has not got to the structural integrity stage, flaking away or recently sprayed and filled. Also worth a look are the jacking points (behind the front wheels and in front of the rears, four in all), which may be rust-stained or unusable.

I found non-threatening rust in the corners of the sunroof opening, on the top lip of the rear wheel apertures, around the license plate (partially remove inner trunk panel to check). Also lift the floor carpeting to see if there is any corrosion around the spare wheel well.

Check around the gas tank and neck junction for corrosion as they often part company at this point and begin to leak when completely full. The gas tanks will also leak along the seam welds when rust pin pricks through, so inspect the floor where the coupe is normally kept, and also look here for rear differential, front transmission and engine oil leaks. You are looking for evidence of major seepage, not worrying about a few spots lost here and there.

Speaking of fluids, have a good look at those (hopefully) in and around the engine. Is the coolant carrying an anti-freeze solution (necessary as a corrosion inhibitor, as well as for its more obvious properties)? Is the oil respectably clean. If it looks virtually unused, does the filter look as though it's been recently changed? Perhaps these items were changed for sale, but were otherwise neglected; judge against the rest of the car to decide.

While under the hood, also inspect the condition of the battery cables, both for evidence of any chafing against the body with potential to start a small fire and the condition of the + and - terminals.

Adjacent to the rear trunk lid button on my CSi there was heavy key damage and subsequent corrosion, and the beginnings of corrosion around the leading edge door hinges—none of that stopped the purchase. However, pronounced rust in the front fenders (back two or three inches from the blinker lights) led me to reduce my bid by some 15 percent, as new fenders were needed to beat the rot permanently.

Up on a ramp is the next stage of inspection. Look for the obvious stuff: any evidence of heavy welding or other substantial repairs? Is the exhaust sound and hung properly to the body? Is there any evidence of scrapes, especially around the sump pan and differential? Is the manual gearbox leaking at the rear? On pre-1980 automatic models a nasty little fire developed if the auto transmission cooler hoses chafed through, so look for evidence of sound fluid lines, especially in the vicinity of any exhaust plumbing.

Repeated evidence of damage or missed maintenance should make you steer clear of the car, however shiny it is on top. Gearbox leaks are common and should simply be put on a "things to do" list.

Unseen in this flattering picture is the light damage and consequent rust around the trunk key lock, whilst the section beneath the rear bumper has also suffered accidental damage and body rot. The rear wheelarches could do with a tidy-up too, but my 635 covered 11,000 miles in 1998 and allowed more sophisticated driving pleasure than any $12,000 alternative.

Picture: Author, June 1998

How it should be: this
brand-new European
1987 coupe brandishes
color-coded plastic end-
plates to the bumpers
and pristine panels.

Picture: BMW Werkfoto,
1987

Are the tires tracking evenly (they are often worn only on the innermost treads, because of the way BMW sets up the suspension)? Some evidence of uneven wear is common, because of tracking defects, but look for
both sides, checking front and rear as a pairing, to show much the same
characteristics. If they do not, look harder for crash damage evidence
(especially hasty over-sprayed paint), as that may be the root cause.

Check for any slop in the steering arms, center link and thrust rod
bushings. On all 5 and 6, through 7 Series, these items are subject to heavy
loads: my 86,000 miler had all the suspension bushings replaced with
stock items, but a more durable fix on the Six is to use bigger bushings
from sources such as the 750, 745 or specialists such as Dinan. Getting to
the source of wear in front or rear of a BMW can be aggravating, and
time-consuming, but would not be a sole reason for dismissing an otherwise interesting and sound coupe.

Now is the time to do some static checks of that complicated control
and dash layout. If there are two of you, one should concentrate on the

engine. Start the engine when cold, and be suspicious of an owner who says "I've warmed it all up for you". You really want to hear a BMW six cylinder start from cold (or as cool as it gets in some States), because the harshest rattles are most evident.

Usually excess noise will be traced to a worn camshaft and rocker set, the result of a design fault that leaves the camshaft starved of lubricant when the banjo fittings on the oil bar have slackened. The car can be driven, but performance will be poor and this will become a priority item with a likely repair cost in the $1000–$1600 range.

A worse cold start fault is more obvious: white smoke that smells sweet. It's not cute, the head is almost certainly cracked and that means major money, whichever way you look at it. If the owner has allowed it to get that far, then the rest of the car is probably not worth rescuing—save as a parts donor.

Check out the operation of all those cockpit functions, especially the unique BMW features such as the Service Interval (SI) indicator, test board lights and (if fitted) on board computer. If the car is being sold as a properly maintained example, expect the majority of SI lights to indicate green, and stay that way for the duration of any test drive. If the SI bat-

The silver dream luxury coupe for $12,000 averages over 22 US mpg, if it is used for more than 10 miles at a time, and there is a majority of major highway use. Otherwise, 17–19 mpg is realistic.

Picture: Author, January 1998

Shortly after all panel-work completed, this 635 found itself tracking rally cars through the forests of Southern Britain. I'm sure American readers know the car on the left is a Volvo wagon, but the little hatchback on the right of "Helga" may be unfamiliar: it's a Czechoslovakian Skoda, a rear engine mark that was a laughing stock (in all but motor rally circles), until Volkswagen absorbed it and started to turn out some fine front-drive product.

Picture: Marilyn Walton, March 1998

teries have expired, this may also lead to wavering readings from the subsidiary water temperature and fuel gauges.

If you are buying cheap and the motor is going to be rebuilt, then know that you can reset these SI units for a lot less than $200 plus quoted at dealerships. Usually, replacing the $5 NiCad batteries will do the trick. Not simple, but not crushingly expensive either, if you are adept enough to utilize some Radio Shack components.

The computer may give a variety of fault-indication readouts (if you are that advanced, you will know to check this out with the aid of a Robert Bentley manual), but be aware that some computers suffer with blown illumination bulbs (two) and work perfectly satisfactorily. This can be checked in strong sunlight. Rectification is then a matter of priorities; even in England I've lived with mine in this state for three months, while the power train and body panels were repaired.

Warning lights tend to matter on this BMW. Aside from the obvious (lack of oil pressure, no alternator charge) the test run may underline that either/both the brake pads are worn away or that the "bomb" or hydraulic pressure accumulator is not accumulating the pressure required to power both brakes and steering.

Expect a good firm brake pedal at varying pressures; the steering should vary with load (assistance is reduced at speed), but do not accept heavy or groaning steering as normal. Chances are that any original BMW of this age will require some steering parts replaced, but if that should include replacing the hydraulic accumulator, then make sure the asking price reflects that fact.

On the road, you are looking for hassle-free progress. The motor should supply seamless power, the temperature gauge should stay in the mid-scale and manual (including clutch action) or automatic transmissions should shift smoothly. If you are not used to manual shifts, the BMW gear change is heavier than a typical Japanese auto, but I'm told it can be eased in most BMW models with an additive like Redline MTL or Amsoil.

The automatic on my 635 was erratic, hunting gears and occasionally missing second from first, but I just chanced that we could fix it with a fluid and filter change. That gamble seems to have paid off with 7000 miles of easy shifting now under our ZF 4-speed belts.

The vexing and frequently debated assortment of front end vibrations should not stop the pruchase of an afflicted coupe, but you could be looking at a variety of causes from worn steering bushings (thrust rods particularly), warped front disk brakes and tired steering box gear. The latter can sometimes be adjusted out, but these are the areas where you need your mechanical sense or a an experienced friend.

Some 90 percent of the problems I experienced here were due to totaled steering bushings and non-aligned tracking. I have to confess I am still chasing an occasional groan on right lock steering and there is too much slack in the system to stop the 220 section tires wandering over most slow speed road cambers. Do better than me on this one, it just did not get done when it should have been a major priority.

There are fundamental safety issues that should be addressed by an official dealership, should you have any subsequent steering concerns. A BMW Service bulletin of November 1987 in the US acknowledges noises emitted by the steering on turning from lock to lock on 6 Series manufactured between 5/82 and 9/87 and says that can be eliminated by installing a 10 mm flat washer, part number 31 11 1 114 348. I have also heard that differing steering location bolts are available, so this is worth checking out as well.

In many US states the performance of the cooling system will be critical. Ensure that any air conditioning unit is functioning correctly. Common California experience seems to be that temperatures up to halfway up the scale are normal, perhaps three quarters if you are creeping though 100 degree traffic with the air on.

There are some larger radiator core fixes you can make, if the performance in this area is unsatisfactory after all routine maintenance items have been checked. On the test run just make sure you leave it running at a standstill for several minutes and that you do simulate traffic running at some point, if only to check out the transmission and cooling.

There's another issue with the braking system that may become apparent in a test run. If the orange ABS (standard on 635CSi) warning light comes on, don't accept that it is a simple bulb malfunction. The ABS really is disconnected and brake performance can then be erratic.

Alternatively the "road runners" among you will know that the light may not appear until you exceed 75–85 mph. The ABS braking will be disconnected until you stop and restart the car using the ignition system. Causes differ: the low speed light usually tells of a failed front wheel sensor, and this can also be activated by turning the steering wheel onto full lock, betraying stretched/severed wiring connection.

The higher speed ABS shutdown is activated by corroded rear wheel hub/ring teeth; the sensors can read to 75–85 mph, but get confused thereafter and shut down the system. I had two hubs/teeth gear sets installed (the parts were the equivalent of $160 in the UK), but the corrosion was so bad that a sensor also had to be replaced (broken on removal) and that cost another $130.

It was nice to get the ABS system back at all speeds (the 635's natural cruising pace is around 95 mph, where it still returns over 25 mpg), but BMW Club members will laugh at the prices quoted, because they will get replacement sensors a lot cheaper, knowing the parts interchangeability from 5 through 6 to 7 Series.

There are many more things that you can check according to your priorities and environment, but I hope I have given you a lead on some of the things I learned the hard way, or that I researched through the generosity of BMW CCA members and their informative web site.

Personal experience

I found out what it was like to own and operate a 6 Series in the nineties. Initially I had wanted a 1972 3.0CS of the previous series, because it was that coupe in white that started the BMW link for me in a 24 hour race. The full restoration experience of intelligent friends with two stablemates (a 3.0CSi and a CSL) put me right off that scheme. I still love that pillarless look and sentiment will drive me into a 3 liter coupe one day, but then

The stock engine bay is workmanlike, rather than a cosmetic attraction, after 93,000 working miles in Britain. Here, the author reflects on an engine that has behaved itself since the top-end replacements were made along with a set of new gas struts to support the forward-hinging hood.

Picture: Courtesy *Classic Cars*. Peter Robain, April 1998

it will be treated as a classic, not used on the regular basis that my 6 Series had to sustain.

When I started searching for a Six in the UK, I learned that what really matters in buying these six cylinder survivors is the condition of the body panels. In the UK, the Sixers offered for sale divide into three categories: doggy inner city debris at dirt cheap prices, half reasonable runners that still need thousands to become regularly reliable choices, and the absolute top dollar collector's pieces. Incidentally, the dollar rates used are those at the time of any purchase and vary from $1.66 to a current $1.60 per £ sterling.

I live 12 miles from BMW's British HQ and there is unnaturally high proportion of 6 Series in daily use, many with the extras (full leather, air conditioning, automatic transmission) that you do not take for granted in Britain. My home village had four such Sixers in daily use, and I soon realized that only the more recent 635s in the care of well-funded business users were likely to be well enough specified and maintained to be a daily driving pleasure in 1997–8 British traffic volumes.

In six months searching through various disappointments—usually with hidden body damage/threatening rust in the fenders and suspension mounting points—I also knew that buying a clean 24-valve M6/M635CSi was out of the question on my budget. Such M-coupes were extremely rare in the UK, just 524 made with right drive steering.

In October 1997, I answered a private ad in *Autocar*, the London-based weekly, for a 1986 BMW 635CSi with low mileage (86,025) and all the extras. These including ZF switchable automatic 4-speed, air conditioning and leather interior. The mileage was properly documented by a BMW Service History to 51,000 miles and the annual UK vehicle test certificates corroborated the annual mileage thereafter.

The price was $1600 (£1000) lower than I had learned was the norm for this specification. I fell in love with its Cosmos Blue lines, Navy blue leather upholstery (with Recaro sports seats up front) and original TRX alloys that had not been curbed (a rarity, believe me).

Caution made me enlist the help of a BMW GB employee to give a second opinion, and that was my best decision. I had spotted the rusty front fenders—blemished beside the front indicators, not in the traditional zone, adjacent to the hood—but I was misled by the clean engine and a four mile test drive into thinking it was mechanically clean. Near-new tires and exhaust, plus some bills for a thrust rod (one side only) from a BMW dealer helped that opinion.

When my BMW friend rang over his findings, I thought that was it: the camshaft had worn the lobes away, he didn't like the operation of the gearbox and "did I know what body panels cost?" The seller was a divorced working lady in her fifties and I was embarrassed to offer her literally thousands under the figure she had named in the advertisement. I would have to slice a third from her price to make it economically viable, should the car have to be sold subsequently.

My inspector named a figure that I should not exceed, bearing in mind the need for $3300 (£2000) in obvious repairs to the fenders and a replacement camshaft. I made a recommended bid of $6400 (£4000), which was promptly accepted. There is a lesson in there...

This made an interesting comparison with the two 635s restored and reported in the February 1998 *Roundel* which had cost their club owners $4800 and $5200 to buy. Both had been radically modified during their rebuilds, so I could not compare subsequent restoration costs. I retained originality while this book was written, my 635 serving as a reminder of how the production stock behaved. The only notable departures from BMW equipment were remote—a door lock/transponder-based anti-theft device(compulsory in Britain, if you want to insure the car affordably) and the use of Avon Turbospeed rather than Michelin TRX tires.

The new acquisition came to our house on a trailer in October 1997. It spent a week lurking in our garage and acquired the code name *Helga* based on its bulging rear end and appetite for liquid refreshment. I felt thoroughly intimidated, especially when I decided to forget my misgivings and take *Helga* out for a drink at the local gas station.

The idea was to get at least enough fuel to get to the official dealer who would do the power train work. My wife aboard our brand new possession, it stalled out at the first set of traffic lights: there was not a glimmer of electronic life. It had to be pushed to safety, having blocked a four-way crossing!

I was at the premature despair stage, not even able to find the hood opening lever (it stays on the left in the right drive conversion). Some minutes pause for thought... I pressed the anti-theft to lock all the doors and walked away to get a breakdown truck. *Helga*'s locks whirred, the anti-theft warnings came on: there was life within.

The combination of fuel tank surge and a number of restarts had shut my 635 down. She was driven straight back to the house and departed from there to the dealership on a trailer once more. *Helga* ascended the trailer courtesy of some old lawn mower fuel, the only leaded gas I had (she runs either leaded 97 octane or super unleaded 98 octane in Euro pre-Cat specification).

BMW original parts were used throughout, a policy I have maintained, because Britain's £/Dm rate was favorable in 1997–98. Also, UK conces-

Despite a size judged as large in Europe and a significant curb weight, the automatic-transmission 635 CSi provides an entertaining country road drive.

Picture: Courtesy *Classic Cars*. Peter Robain, April 1998

sions were made in service and parts supply through official channels to owners of older (more than four years) BMWs. This was to offset the success of specialists in emptying out the service bays of any official BMW dealer for cars no longer under warranty, which was expanded in 1996 to last three years instead of twelve months.

Helga came under my local dealership scrutiny to see how many other things were wrong. She had the minor problems that I had expected, in addition to the rear discs and main steering tie rod needing replacement. I celebrated by ordering an Inspection 1 service, for even the emergency red service light was jammed on.

I got my gorgeous coupe back 12 days later. *Helga* was immaculately cleaned, but with no fuel (still, despite two requests), no stamp in the service book (rectified three months later) and a huge pall of blue smoke on turnover. The latter turned out to be the exhaust gasket replacements experiencing their first taste of heat (so, it had apparently not been road tested to working temperatures).

After most of a month's ownership I had traveled about 0.75 of a mile and was determined to see what I had gotten myself into, blue smoke or no blue smoke! A Sunday morning jaunt of 20 miles established that the dealership bill of more than $1760 (£1100) had been an investment, the unit sounding as though it had just been run-in and not a trace of smoke to be seen once she had slept overnight.

In the ensuing 3000 miles, the motor has been one of the outstanding pleasures of ownership: I did not use more than 3000 rpm for the first 500 miles after the new camshaft ($465/£275) and its attendant rockers were installed, but now it is asked to work up to 6200 occasionally and is deeply impressive.

This 3.4 liter six pre-dates catalytic converters in Europe. Thus it hauls in horizons with light plane speed (without the noise, needing only 3000 rpm for 97 mph) over motorway mileage. It also has a much more civilized cabin than any light plane.

A month later I had braced myself for a visit to a local body shop (Mercedes and Volkswagen approved), whose labor rate was almost half that of the official BMW dealership. I was armed with new front fenders, a replacement center section to the rear bumper, a fitting kit for the rumpled rear end, including the rubber inserts and mounting bolts (which had all rusted beyond use). At that time the official UK price of the fenders was $879 (£520) apiece. Some intense negotiating within the BMW network brought the panels down to under $500 apiece.

The fenders were replaced, along with yet another steering link (between the previous owner and myself, every link, bushing and front end tie rod has now been replaced inside 12 months), this time it was the drop link anti-roll bar connection and ball joint that needed replacement.

The body bill was £283 for labor, £122 for paint, but now the exchange rate had shifted to the $1.65 region per £ sterling so that meant a labor total of $668 (£527), exclusive of UK taxes of 17.5percent. I had spent a total $10,693 (£6560.16) on the 635CSi, parts and repairs, which left me around £500 within my $11,410 (£7000) budget.

After two months of ownership spent mainly in garages, I turned my attention to sort out two long-running problems. Both were safety-related. The steering groaned on right-hand lock and fed back varying vibrations through an optional sports three spoke leather wheel. Also, at precisely 84 indicated mph, the ABS warning light would illuminate and the ABS anti-lock braking system would be terminated, absent until such time as the ignition was turned off and the car restarted.

The steering links having all been replaced (this highly stressed system is a weak link in any eighties 5, 6 or 7 Series), I took the car to a local specialist and went for the full tracking and wheel-balancing routine. It certainly needed a lot of correction, but too late to save the innermost tread on the rear 220 section Avons, which had covered less than 4000 miles. The rear tires were replaced with Avon equipment some 3000 miles later.

New rear ABS hubs and their inbuilt sensor teeth was a piece of remote troubleshooting suggested by my BMW contact and it proved correct. It also reduced the vibration mentioned before, but I do not think I am going to have the vibration problems beaten without more attention to the steering gear. At present it is one of those problems that clears magically, and then comes back with a vengeance for no apparent reason, but balanced *rear* wheels and tires helped.

Some 11 days after the wheels had been balanced and the front end metal finished, an Amtrak panel van entered my life. It reversed into the front end of the legally-parked BMW, setting off the alarm. I ran out of adjacent offices to earnestly discuss this matter with the van driver, who had been "blinded by the sun". Unfortunately the external knuckle hinge of the van's back door ripped into the 'beak' of the BMW and damaged that pristine front end to the tune of $2140 (£1400): all this at less than 10 mph!

I was pretty downhearted by this. We lost the use of the car for the best part of a month, right over the Christmas break, when it would normally have been working for a living. Then, when the guys at my local panel shop had it back together, one of their staff dropped a bumper on a

You can take this 12-year-old anywhere. The 635 visits a major Ferrari specialist near Heathrow Airport. The BMW finds the only parking slot is next to the owner's winter driver: a Bentley Turbo.

Picture: Marilyn Walton, December 1997

Classic coupe action. The 635 soaks up some more miles with elegant ease. A former GM employee has a similar coupe, domiciled in Spain, that seems equally happy to gallop with more than 200,000 miles recorded...and no major hardware replacements.

Picture: Peter Robain, April 1998

repainted panel, scratched it deeply, and had to start over on that sector of the battered BMW!

I got *Helga* back in the dead time between Christmas 1997 and New Year 1998. We had done just about 1200 miles together in less than three months. I was determined we would rack up some miles per dollar/ pound spent.

Our first job as a reunited couple was fabulous: an interview at a superb Ferrari specialist (Talacrest of Egham, Surrey, just about 15 miles from London Heathrow airport, worth a visit). The 635 proved almost as long as the owner's winter transport (Bentley Turbo V8) and a lot more fun to drive.

Heartened by this encouraging preliminary to 1998, I looked forward to more mileage drifting across Britain when the traffic was heavy, or the exhilaration of instant power from the classic 6-cylinder BMW motor. Amazing grip with 220 section rubber was an unexpected rolling country road pleasure, but the grip on wet or icy urban streets is notable chiefly for its absence in a world full of grippier front drive formats. It desperately needs a limited slip differential, but that was only standard equipment on M-coupes in Britain.

I usually opt for electronic gearshift control (which also has the useful facility to raise rpm shift points in Sports mode), rather than the mechanical shift. The lever control is so stiff that I only use it for the first start or long traffic waits; the auto shift was criticized in the independent road tests of the eighties, and American sources did not seem to like the Getrag manual gearboxes fitted prior to M6.

Smaller routine tasks that I tackled myself included refurbishing all the leather trim. That was a satisfying day/overnight manual task, using Connolly cleaner, leather food and polish products. There is still a small tear to rectify in the vulnerable side bolster of the sports seat, just where the driver regularly eases over it .

Other smaller problems I tackled included the screenwashers and front wipers jamming on. That emptied the screenwasher fluid and drove me mad with its continual buzzing over a long and slow journey in snow. I also repeatedly relocated the rear trunk trim on its Dzus fasteners and mourned the lack of the fabled tool kit, long since robbed.

The big annual trial for any vehicle over four years old (since first registration) in the UK is the Ministry of Transport (MoT) certification test. No MoT certificate, no public road use. The MoT used to be a bad joke

"Das BMW Coupe— ein Klassiker up to Date" was the BMW press office's Anglo-German title to this study. Whatever the language, I am sorry to leave this tale of the coupe that made a motoring writer dig into his own pockets to try and understand the magic Munich wove into a simple, yet refined automobile.

Picture: BMW Werkfoto, 1987

carried out in the time it took to write the (often stolen) certificate slip, but in the nineties the test has become a 40 minute search that leans toward a genuine full safety and (very loose) emissions check.

At the close of January 1998, *Helga* returned a third time to her body shop and passed the MoT in 45 minutes. But we had greater ambitions, fixing the screenwashers (blocked by local limescale and still not 100 percent) and entrusting the replacement of those previously purchased ABS rear-end toothed hubs. Sounded comparatively simple and one side "just fell apart and reassembled, no bother at all" according to the expat New Zealander boss.

When they tackled the other side, corrosion had welded all the locking washers together and an ABS sensor was damaged beyond repair in trying to lift it from its rusty home. Although I had bought the brace of new ABS toothed hubs at discount, a replacement Bosch wheel sensor was simply bought retail ($130/£78). At the end of 5 hours wrestling the total bill (including that annual MoT charge) was almost $500/£300, about ten times what a straight MoT certification would require. But it was worth it...

Now I could take advantage of the 635's higher speed abilities without losing the ABS back-up system, and some of the persistent vibrations had totally disappeared. Now my CSi was capable of casually cruising at the same sort of speeds and distances as would be normal in a current $80,000/£50,000 BMW 7-Series or the Jaguar V8s.

The 12 year old BMW is no match for the silence, body strength and aerodynamic excellence of the current Jaguar or BMW breed, but for a total £6848.99/$11,027 the 635 gives me budget pleasure. I prefer its cleanly styled and comfortable cabin to the sanitized current machinery.

At least I prefer the ambiance of 635CSi refreshed leather and the clearest instrumentation devised until it comes to crash test time. Then, I'll take any current prestige product for head-butting walls or other vehicles, thank you.

Appendix 1

German Production and US sales

All figures courtesy of BMW AG, based on 1992 and 1996 production records.

Total production, all types,1976–1989

Model	Production span	Total produced
628CS	6/79 to 5/88	5950
630CS (**US 630CSi**)	2/76 to 8/77 (9/76 to 8/77)	5766 (1794)
633CSi (**US 633CSi**)	1/76 to 2/84 (1/78 to 9/84)	23,432 (11,939)
635CSi (**US 635CSi/L6**)	6/78 to 4/89 (10/84 to 4/89)	45,213 (13,002)
M635CSi/M6) (**US M6**)	4/84 to 4/89 (10/86 to 9/88)	5,855 (1,767)
Total 6 Series **produced**	1/76 to 4/89 (9/76 to 4/89)	86,216 (US: 28,502)

Collector's notes

I stress that these are official manufacturing figures, not sales units. This means that the figures take no account of gray imports into the US, and these could considerably alter the total number of M6 machines resident in the States, as well as the total number of 635CSis in European trim. As they stand, the US accounted for one third or 33 percent of all 6 Series output.

For perspective, know that just 28,292 of the 8 Series were made from 1989 to 1996, and production levels were slipping in 1996...right down to a third of the 6 Series production total in its last full year.

Total production of the earlier (sometimes E9-coded) coupes of 1965–75 was 44,237, so the 6 Series is the most successful big BMW coupe manufactured to fit the traditional luxury niche. However, it was not the biggest-selling BMW coupe of all. The smaller E36 3 Series, from 316 to M3, is the company's high-volume coupe: these remained in production for most of the 1990s.

The official US import "M6" with the S38 24-valve engine was rated 256 bhp at 6,500 rpm, some 30 bhp down from the European version. The US variant entered production in November 1986 and was terminated in September 1988 when 1,767 had been manufactured. This made the US the second-largest group of buyers after European left-hand-drive shipments of 3,283.

The rarest production year for the US "M6" model is 1988, when only 318 were built.

The rarest US model year for the 635 is also 1988, when 185 were manufactured.

The rarest model shipped to the US is the 630CSi. It had the smallest total production of any variant (5,766) and shipments to US specification (all fuel-injected, where European cars were then carbureted) were measured in hundreds. Some 862 came in 630CSi catalytic converter specification for the 1977 model year. Then 496 were made to US specs, so a total of 1,358 were made to meet American requirements in the production years 1976–77.

US Sales

Late in the production of this title, BMW North America released amended sales figures for their home market. This left us little time to update the relevant chapters, but was obviously vital to understanding the production figures, thus their presence here. Our thanks to Andrew Culter, Corporate Communications, for ensuring we received statistics the author had not seen published previously.

Note that the 6 Series was made in Germany from 1976 to 1989, when the 850 range was meant to replace all 6 Series.

Overall US 6 Series sales, 1977-1992

Year	US sales
1977	1,079
1978	992
1979	838
1980	1,190
1981	1,138
1982	1,515
1983	2,613
1984	2,697
1985	3,824
1986	2,979
1987	2,532
1988	1,529
1989	837
1990	259
1991	12
1992	5
TOTAL	24,039

6 Series sales by model & calendar year

Year	Model	Sales
1977	630CSi	1,079
1978	630CSi	531
	633CSi	461
	TOTAL	992
1979	630CSi	39
	633CSi	799
	TOTAL	838
1980	630CSi	2
	633CSi	1,188
	TOTAL	1,190
1981	633CSi	1,138
1982	633CSi	1,515
1983	633CSi	2,613
1984	633CSi	2,612
	635CSi	85
	TOTAL	2,697
1985	633CSi	296
	635CSi	3,528
	TOTAL	3,824

Year	Model	Sales
1986	633CSi	8
	635CSi	2,971
	TOTAL	2,979
1987	635CSi	727
	M6	588
	L6	1,217
	TOTAL	2,532
1988	635CSi	761
	M6	666
	L6	102
	TOTAL	1,529
1989	635CSi	473
	M6	354
	L6	10
	TOTAL	837
1990	635CSi	251
	M6	7
	L6	1
	TOTAL	259
1991	635/M6/L6	12
1992	635/M6/L6	5

Appendix 2

6 Series Performance Statistics

Figures given here are not those of the manufacturer. They are averaged from independently timed sources in relevant markets: US, UK, and Germany.

European specification 6 Series

Model	Year Tested	Power (bhp)	Weight (lbs)
628 CSi	1980	184	3,197
633 CSi	1976	200	3,280
635 CSi	1984	218	3,225
M635 CSi	1984	286	3,325

US specification 6 Series

Model	Year Tested	Power (bhp)	Weight (lbs)
630 CSi	1977	176	3,510
633 CSi	1978	177	3,500
635 CSi	1985	182	3,375
M6	1987	256	3,570

Model	0-30 mph (secs)	0-60 mph (secs)	0-100 mph (secs)	1/4 mile (secs)	Test UK
628 CSi	3.0	8.5	24.0	16.1	19.8
633 CSi	2.8	8.0	22.0	14.9 @ 83 mph	21.0
635 CSi	2.5	7.0	19.0	15.5 @ 90 mph	22.0
M635 CSi	2.3	6.0	15.5	14.5 @ 98 mph	17.5

Model	0-30 mph (secs)	0-60 mph (secs)	0-100 mph (secs)	1/4 mile (secs)	Test US
630 CSi	3.3	10.0	32.0	17.5 @ 81 mph	18.0
633 CSi	2.8	8.3	27.5	16.8 @ 85 mph	18.0
635 CSi	2.5	8.1	24.5	16.0 @ 85 mph	17.0
M6	2.5	6.8	17.0	15.4 @ 85 mph	15.5

Appendix 3

Factory-backed 6 Series Achievements

From the 1960s to the 1990s, BMW has provided the sedan-racing benchmark against which others must measure up in all but NASCAR.

The BMW company and privateer/works-assisted record in the European Championship is unlikely to ever be matched, since the European series was cancelled after the 1988 edition, following 25 years of championship endurance racing across some of Europe's toughest tracks.

No rival matches BMW's sedan record of 16 European and one World Championship title, 1966–88. You can add all the opposition up and still not exceed the BMW winning record of outright victory in 20 editions of the 33 Spa Francorchamps 24-hour races held between 1964–97.

The 6 Series contributions to this magnificent record are highlighted below, first by championship titles, then by the most prestigious race results for factory-backed racers.

6 Series achievements

Year	Driver	Model	Title
1980	Herbie Werginz Harald Neger	Group 2 3.5 635 CSi	Vallelunga, Rome winners, I
1980	Herbie Werginz Harald Neger	Group 2 3.5 635 CSi	Monza 4 hours winners, I
1980	Umberto Grano Harald Neger Herbie Werginz	Group 2 3.5 635 CSi	Tourist Trophy Silverstone, UK winners
1981	Helmut Kelleners Umberto Grano	Group 2 3.5 635 CSi	European Champions
1983	Heyer A. Hahne Tassin	Group A 635 CSi Juma	Spa 24 hours winners, B
1983	BMW Factory drivers	Group A 635 CSi	six European Championship qualifying races
1983	Dieter Quester	Group A 3.5 635 CSi	European Champion
1984	Alain Cudini Danny Snobeck	Group AS 635 CSi Snobeck	Vallenunga winners
1984	Private and factory- backed drivers	635	wins three European Championship races
1985	Roberto Ravaglia Berger Surer	Group A 635 CSi Schnitzer	Spa 24 hours, B Schnitzer 635 also 2nd
1986	Roberto Ravaglia	Group A 3.5 635 CSi	European Champion and four Euro rounds
1986	Dieter Quester Heger Tassin	Group A 635 CSi Schnitzer	Spa 24 hours and BMW 1-5 winners including 325i

Appendix 4

Collectible 6 Series Specifications

Model	US 633 CSi	Euro 633 CSi	US 635 CSi
Year chosen	1978	1976	1985
Years made	1978-84	1976-84	1984-89*
Motor type	SOHC 12v	SOHC 12v	SOHC 12v
Capacity	3,210 cc	3,210 cc	3,430 cc
Compression ratio	8.4:1	9.0:1	8.0:1
Bore & stroke	89 x 86 mm	89 x 86 mm	92 x 86 mm
Injection type	L-Jetronic	L-Jetronic	Bosch Motronic
Bhp/torque (lb. ft.@ rpm)	177/196 5,500/4,000	200/210 5,500/4,250	182/214 5,400/4,000
Gearbox	4-speed manual 3-speed auto, ZF	4-speed manual 3-speed auto, ZF	5-speed manual 4-speed auto, ZF
Final drive ratio	3.45:1	3.25:1	3.45:1
Wheels and tires	6.5 x 14 195/70 HR 14	6.0 x 14 195/70 VR 14	6.5 x 15.4 220/55 VR
Independent curb weight (lbs)	3,400	3,280	3,375
Front/rear ratio	55/45	57/43	55/45
Maximum speed (mph)	124	131	125

*This model available earlier in Europe only as the 1978–82 3.5-liter

Figures given here are averaged from independent sources in US, UK, and Germany. Independent curb weight is a non-manufacturer figure.

Model	Euro 635 CSi	US M6	Euro M635 CSi	Group A racer
Year chosen	1984	1985	1984	1983
Years made	1982-89	1986-88	1984-89	1983-86
Motor type	SOHC 12v	DOHC 24v	DOHC 24v	SOHC 12v
Capacity	3,430 cc	3,453 cc	3,453 cc	3,475 cc
Compression ratio	10.0:1	9.8:1	10.5:1	11.0:1
Bore & stroke	92 x 86 mm	93.4 x 84 mm	93.4 x 84 mm	92.6 x 86 mm
Injection type	L-Jetronic	Bosch Motronic	Bosch Motronic	Bosch L-Jetronic
Bhp/torque (lb. ft.@ rpm)	218/228 5,200/4,000	256/243 6,500/4,500	286/251 6,500/4,500	285/257 6,000/5,500
Gearbox	5-speed manual 4-speed auto, ZF	5-speed manual	5-speed manual	5-speed manual racing ratios and "dog-leg" shift
Final drive ratio	3.07:1	3.91:1 Std LSD @ 25%	3.73:1 Std LSD	3.07 to 3.91 75% LSD
Wheels and tires	6.5 x 15.4 220/55 VR	7.0 x 16 240/45 VR	8.0 x 16.4 240/45 VR 415	11.0 x 16
Independent curb weight (lbs)	3,225	3,570	3,460	2,607 ballasted 2,554 no ballast
Front/rear ratio	56/44	52/48	53/47	N/A
Maximum speed (mph)	138	145	150	165

Appendix 5

Racing Chassis–Numbers and Clients

The big production years were 1983 (RA1 prefix in all but two cases) and 1984 (RA2 prefix to serial number). The country designations are international, but you need to know that ETCC stands for European Touring Car Championship, BTCC is the British Championship, and DTM is the German national series (Deutsche Tourenwagen Meisterschaft).

BMW Motorsport racing bodies and hardware 1983–88

Chassis #	Client	Country	Programme/drivers
E24 AAA-01*	Works Proto/ Cheylesmore BMW	D/UK	BTCC/Hans Stuck
E24 RA2-01	Eggenberger	CH	ETCC/Kelleners/Grano
E24 RA1-02**	BMW Australia/ F.Gardner	Aus	National title/Richards
E24 RA1-03	BMW France	F	National
E24 RA1-04	BMW France	F	National
E24 RA1-05	BMW France	F	National
E24 RA1-06	BMW France	F	National
E24 RA1-07	Factory/Schnitzer	D	ETCC/Stuck-Queste
E24 RA1-08	Eggenberger	CH	ETCC/Briozzo
E24 RA1-09	Eggenberger	CH	ETCC/Stalder

* AAA-01 was crashed heavily but was reborn in a new body
** RA1 was re-used as a test and spcial development car and had a later life in the hands of CC Racing for BMW GB in national series

BMW Motorsport racing bodies and hardware 1983–88 (continued)

Chassis #	Client	Country	Programme/drivers
E24 RA1-10	Juma/Belgian National	B	ETCC/Heyer-Hahne
E24 RA1-11	Juma/Belgian National	B	ETCC/Xhenceval-Bourgoigne
E24 RA1-12	König	D	DTM
E24 RA1-13	Leopold von Bayern	D	DTM: Stuck/Brun
E24 RA1-14	V.B. Racing	CS	ETCC/Strycek
E24 RA1-15	Delcour	B	ETCC/Spa 24 hours
E24 RA1-16	BMW Ag	D	Show Car/retained
E24 RA1-17	Gartlan/Grace	UK	National/Sytner
E24 RA1-18	BMW France	F	National
E24 RA1-19	BMW France	F	National
E24 RA1-20	BMW France	F	National
E24 RA1-21	Hartge tuning [D]	D	ETCC/ DTM
E24 RA1-22	BMW France	F	National
E24 RA1-23	Hartge tuning [D]	B/F	ETCC/DTM/nationals
E24 RA1-24			
E24 RA1-25	Faltz of Essen	D	DTM
E24 RA2-26*	BMW Belgium	B	Unknown
E24 RA2-27		D	ETCC
E24 RA2-28	ASP Racing	CH	Concept Car project
E24 RA2-29	Cheyles more BMW	GB	BTCC

* Chassis numbers were changed to RA2 series from 1984 onward

(continued on next page)

BMW Motorsport racing bodies and hardware 1983–88 (continued)

Chassis #	Client	Country	Programme/drivers
E24 RA2-30	Circuiti/Opptyhauss		
E24 RA2-31	Factory/Schnitzer	D	ETCC/ DTM.
E24 RA2-32			
E24 RA2-33	Polak Racing	US	
E24 RA2-34	Factory/Schnitzer	D	ETCC Original Teile livery
E24 RA2-35	Factory/Schnitzer	D	ETCC Originale Teile livery
E24 RA2-36	Eggenberger Racing	CH	ETCC
E24 RA2-37	BMW GB/CC Racing	GB	BTCC/Weaver
E24 RA2-38	Eggenberger Racing	CH	ETCC
E24 RA2-39	BMW GB/CC Racing	GB	BTCC/ Woodman
E24 RA2-40	Eggenberger Racing	CH	ETCC
E24 RA2-41	Eggenberger Racing	CH	ETCC
E24 RA2-42	Hartge tuning	D	ETCC
E24 RA2-43	Hartge turning	D	ETCC
E24 RA2-44	BMW Australia/ Gardner	Aus	National title winner/Richards
E24 RA2-45	Obermaier	D	DTM
E24 RA2-46	Gartlan Racing/Grace	GB	Group N, not A. Crashed by B.Williams, rebuilt & sold to NZ
E24 RA2-47	Juma Racing	B	ETCC
E24 RA2-48	Juma Racing	B	ETCC
E24 RA2-49		D	DTM

Appendix 6

Production Notes

The following is a basic listing of the major model breaks and changes for 1976–90 American (US) and European 6 Series cars. Although the models were similar in outward appearance for long periods of time, there were many small detail changes both inside and outside. For example, between 1987 and 1988 E28 6 Series the only exterior clues to the model year change are that the '87 model year had "bulging" front parking lamp lenses and much longer bumper return trim along the sides. I have not tried to identify every change, but have grouped the models under their years with the most significant details noted.

US Models

630 CSi
Made 9/76 to 8/77.

1977 model year	Motor of 2985cc/176 bhp. Bosch L-Jetronic with thermal reactor catalytic converter
	US 5 m.p.h. bumpers, no rear wrap-around. Length up six inches compared to European specs
	Choice of 4-speed manual by Getrag or 3-speed ZF HP22 automatic gearbox
	Multi spoke 6 x 14 inch alloys with 195/70 HR (not VR) Michelin XVS
	Limited slip differential optional
	140 m.p.h. speedometer
	The smallest number of units shipped into the US

US Models (continued)

633 CSi
Manufactured from 1/78 to 9/84, 49-States specification.

1978–79 model years

Motor of 3210cc/177 bhp with Bosch L-Jetronic, compatible with 91 RON unleaded gas, and thermal reactor catalytic converter

Wheels were 6.5 x 14 BBS with 195/70 VR Michelins

US 5 mph bumpers, as per 630 CSi

Showroom sticker included metallic paint, four-speaker AM/FM stereo radio/cassette, electric slide and tilt two-way roof, air conditioning, and leather trim

Options included 3-speed ZF automatic ($290) and limited slip differential by ZF ($530)

1980 model year

Oxygen sensor, three-way catalytic converter

1982–83 model years

Bumpers (rear) extended to rear of rear arches

TRX wheel and tire option became standard

5-Speed manual transmission standard. Auto option came with cruise control

Red readout digital clock, 85 m.p.h. speedometer

Central locking updated with passenger door and trunk lock control

Ignition key light fitted

US Models (continued)

635 CSi
Manufactured to US specification from 10/84 to 9/89

1985 model year

Motor of 3430cc/ 182 bhp with Bosch Motronic management

US bumpers add 6.5 inches to European length

Front spoiler only, integrated auxiliary lights. Rear trunk carries chrome identifier, 635 CSi

6.5 x 15.4 inch alloy TRX wheels with 220/55VR tires

Showroom equipment included leather trim, power seat adjustment, cruise control, three-spoke steering wheel; nine function computer, BMW four-speaker, 13 watt per channel stereo radio/cassette

Optional ZF 4-speed automatic ($795) and Limited slip differential ($390)

February 1987 production changes

Rebadged L6 for US market. Manufactured to 1989 but sold up to 1990–91 in limited numbers

Motor of 32430Cc/182 bhp

Showroom with 4-speed ZF 4-sped automatic transmission, no limited slip differential

No rear spoiler, no front L 6 badge; used 635 front air dam with integrated auxiliary lights

Showroom included ABS brakes

TRX wheel and tire specification standard

1988 model year

Motor to European 735i specs, still 3430cc but 208 bhp

1989 model year

CD changer option added

Power steering adapted from 7 Series

US Models (continued)

M6

Imported 1987–89 European M635 CSi as M6 with detuned engine

February 1987 production changes

DOHC motor with 24-valves had 3453cc/256 bhp with Bosch Motronic management and three-way catalytic converter

Manual transmission, H pattern, 5-speed only, limited slip differential

BBS 7.7 x 16.3 inch three-piece wheels with 240/45 VR 415 Michelin tires

US bumpers. Front and rear spoilers to later European specs

M6 badge front grille and rear trunk; color-coded mirrors

Showroom equipment included leather trim, power/memory seats, air conditioning; two-way tilt andslide sunroof, nine-function computer, cruise control, anti-lock (ABS) brakes of larger diameters, AM/FM stereo radio/cassette with eight speakers

European Models

630 CS

For LHD Continental Europe only. Only manufactured from 2/76 to 8/77

1976–77 model years   Motor of 2985cc/185 bhp with Solex 4-barrel carburetor

Wheels were 6J x 14 H2 multi spoke alloys (as Euro 633) wear 195/70 VR Michelin XWX

Trunk badge, right side read 630 CS (no "i" on this Euro model only: US spec car is badged 630 CSi)

Small chrome and rubber inlay European bumpers

Standard equipment included analog central clock within twist ring; 7-light (green) System Check, four electric windows with tinted glass and four vented disk brakes

Choice of manual (4-speed) or Automatic 3-speed (ZF HP 22)

European Models (continued)

633 CSi

Manufactured from 1/76 to 2/84. On Sale: LHD 9/76; UK RHD 10/76. UK Chassis start at 4380001 (Manual) and 4390001 (Automatic). The last UK RHD 633CSi was Chassis # 4381133.

1976–81 model years	Motor of 3210cc/200 bhp with Bosch L-Jetronic. No catalytic converter
	Trunk badge, right side, 633 CSi
	Euro chrome and rubber bumpers
	Shared wheel and tire specification with 630CS
	140 mph speedometer (UK), 240 km/h European LHD
	Optional 5-speed with dog-leg first gear offered all Euro 6 Series from 630 to M635
1982 model year	Dash revised to include digital (red readouts) clock, revised heating and ventilation controls and speedometer rev counter flanking central water temperature and fuel gauge (rectangular instead of original single pane panel to left of larger speedo/tachometer)
January 1983 production changes	ZF 4-speed automatic transmission available
1984 model year	ZF 4HP-22 Switchable (Sport/Economy) automatic available, still 4-speed with lock-out clutch for direct overdrive 4th

European Models (continued)

635 CSi

Manufactured from 6/78 to 4/89. On sale European LHD 7/78. UK RHD was available by 12/78 at chassis # 5550001.

1978–81 model years	Motor of 3453cc/218 bhp with Bosch L-Jetronic. No catalytic converter
	Front and rear spoilers, front with stripes, rear in solid rubber wrapped around
	Roundel badge. Body side stripe with thicker lower section
	Trunk badge 635 CSi inlaid into black rubber rear spoiler
	Twin exhausts of two-inch diameter (bore of 630/633 is 1.65 in)
	Cast alloy "Spider's Web" wheels, 6.5 x 13 inches with 195/70 Michelin XDX initial
	RHD and 205/70 VR 14 option subsequently standard on same BBS style wheel 160 mph speedometer (RHD) or 260 km/h LHD and four-spoke steering wheel with individual horn buttons (as per 630/633)
1982 model year	Dash revised to include digital (red readouts) clock, revised heating and ventilation controls and speedometer rev counter flanking central water temperature and fuel gauge (rectangular instead of original single pane panel to left of larger speedo/tachometer)
June 1982 (approximately) production changes	Motor of smaller 3430cc/218 bhp
	Digital Motor Electronics (DME)
	New TRX/Michelin wheel and tyre equipment (6.5 x 15.4 in with 220/55 VR 390 Michelin TRX tires) with standard ABS anti-lock braking
	Three-Spoke steering wheel, more padding, 2 horn button
	Econometer inset into speedometer
	Service Interval Indicator adopted
	Wrap-around rear bumpers for Europe and UK extended to rear of wheel arch

(635 CSi continued on next page)

European Models (continued)

635 CSi

(Continued)

January 1983
production changes   ZF 4-speed automatic transmission available

1983 model year   New rear spoiler is thinner, inverted u-shape and badges no longer inset. Front spoiler has cavities to carry auxiliary lamps (changes not simultaneous, rear first)

1984–86 model years   ZF 4HP-22 Switchable (Sport/Economy) automatic available, still 4-speed with lock-out clutch for direct overdrive 4th. Electronic control system linked to Bosch DME of motor

1987 model year   Endcaps in plastic wraps matched body color, to give US similar appearance to shrouded chrome 2.5 mph smaller European bumpers

Rear spoiler color matched deck section of trunk, rubber inlay wrap-around section aft, straight line across trunk lid, except Roundel badge indent

1988 model year   Motor to European 735i specs, still 3430cc but 220 bhp and unleaded gas UK / catalytic converter capabilities for Germany

Bosch Motronic management

Climate Control air conditioning standard

Self-leveling system for rear suspension

Uprated headlamps, ellipsoid

Standardized 7.7 x 16.3 BBS (ex-M6) wheels with 240/45 VR 415 TRXs

Some UK RHD 1988–89 models incorporated a Highline standard specification with US-style luxury items (leather, air, power seats with memory etc.) marketed in one extra cost package that adds up to $3000 to pre-owned used car values a decade later

European Models (continued)

M635 CSi

Manufactured from 4/84 to 4/89. German LHD press launch cars were hand-built from late 1983 onward. UK availability in RHD by 2/85. Three types of shift lever badge were fitted to Euopean cars, but the exact breakdon is unknown. Those badges are 1) M tri-colors with shift pattern, 2) M emblem with chrome surround and no shift pattern, 3) M tri-colors, M emblem, and shift pattern.

1984–88 model years
Twin-cam 24-valve motor of 3453cc/286 bhp replaced previous SOHC 12v designs. Cast valve/rockers cover carried BMW letters initially, MPower for US and later eighties European models

///M badge front grille and rear trunk, not M6 or M635 CSi, just M and ///colors

Front and rear spoilers, front extended over 635 by ribbed matte black section. Rear as contemporary 635 CSi

Color coded door mirrors, three-spoke steering wheel with M-colors and M-badge inset to tachometer. initial 1983–84 European test cars from Munich with dog-leg first Getrag sports 5-speed shift pattern. Conventional H pattern standard by 1985

Showroom wheels and tires were 165 TR 390 with 220/50 VR 390 Michelin TRX. Option (widely fitted and utilized for press cars) was 210 TR 415 BBS 3-piece with Michelin 240/45 VR 415 TRX

Battery located in trunk

1989 model year
BBS wheels standard with 240/45VR 415s

Plastic bumper side sections on 2.5 mph Euro chrome units

Color-coded rear spoiler with rubber inset. Color coded mirrors throughout M6/635 CSi

Ellipsoid headlamps

Powered leather seats, air conditioning and other American features incorporated as standard

Some indication of a special run of "Motorsports Edition" models, with 292 bhp, achieved by reworking manifolds and engine management

Index

Acknowledgments

Researching period pictures, buying my own 6 Series (a decade after its production demise), have added to the pleasures of putting this title together. I hope you enjoy the result as much as I did its creation in trans-atlantic association with Michael Bentley, John Kittredge, Lee Ann Best, Albert Dalia, and the team at Robert Bentley Publishers.

Significant Others

I must sincerely thank: Claudi Hoepner-Korinth (now international press officer at BMW AG.); Susannah Reynolds-Britze (BMW Motorsport Press Department); Michael Schimpke now at Porsche); Peter Zöllner (Archiv, retired); Dieter Stappert (former BMW Motorsport manager), and Uwe Mahla, later BMW's national press manager.

Back in 1983, Raymond Playfoot and Michele Cory lent me a 635CSi that took me and colleague Peter Newton (now a PR Executive with Fiat-Alfa Romeo group) around the original 1700 miles of German research, on British roads. All in such smooth style that it left the 15 year ambition to own my own Six, now realized.

A trip to Munich with Malcolm Gartlan (UK race entrant) and 6 Series technical wizard Ted Grace resulted in the purchase of a racing Group A 635. We attempted to put Steve Soper in such a racing BMW, some five seasons before the deed was done—at the time of writing Mr. Soper is still racing BMW product.

Thanks to subsequent Ford motorsport chief Martin Whitaker, I was privileged to drive BMW dealership Cheylesmore's factory specification 635CSi Group A competitor. This the 285 bhp coupe so spectacularly raced by Hans Joachim Stuck in Britain.

In the nineties BMW AG. in Munich and its satellites in the USA and UK contributed significantly. Most expertise came from the BMW historic Archiv, now superbly re-housed within the four floors of Mobile Tradition. These official archives, under the genial managerial control of Heinrich Klebl, provided over half the illustrations in association with Karin Ammach. The balance of pictures are from the amazing library of *Roundel's* chief photographer, Klaus Schnitzer, my own UK/USA pictorial work, or drawn from my UK files.

I learned much during a 1998 flying visit to Mobile Tradition/Archiv's new home, right next door to the Fiz Engineering Center of Fiz, Munich City. I spent happy hours on other floors of what was a converted stores bought by BMW for its appropriate ambiance and sheer space in the nineties.

Mobile Tradition's author Walter Zeichner, the Mobile Tradition Managing Director Christian Eich, and old friend, Dirk Strassl (Communication Director), were my guides. There are three racing 635s on the top floor, and excellent examples of the breed below, so the journey could have been justified on this basis alone.

I spent just as much time admiring motorcycles and productions cars that I had never seen in the metal. Plus a racing Z3 that it was forbidden to photograph, but whose inflated cartoon-lines made it the most striking BMW never to take to the track.

At BMW NA Rob Mitchell's US product knowledge is unmatched, whilst Chris Willows (UK Press Relations Manager) and Alun Parry at BMW GB, eased the pain of producing a new title on an obsolete model. Alun's knowledge of older BMWs aided me to own and operate my own 635CSi, adding a unique dimension to the text.

Local friends who progressed the pleasure of 6 Series ownership included Alistair McArthur of Wargrave Coachworks, fellow 635 CSi owners expat Arizonians Mike and Sandy Donohue, and then Landlords of the White Hart Hotel, Keith and Mary Brinsden. Mary endured hours of car talk as qualified engineer Keith guided me through the practicalities of older car ownership, for Keith was then restoring a 7.2 liter Chrysler V8-engined Jensen.

Keith's courtesy allowed all the Connolly leather products I needed to reinvigorate the beautiful blue leather of my 635CSi. A task that gave me considerable pleasure.

Factually, I drew earlier information either from the original publication, or added to that material through the accessible format of the Brookland Books title *BMW 6 Series Gold Portfolio, 1976-89.* Or stepped outside and had a look at what BMW had done to manufacture my coupe in association with Karman.

Manufacturing statistics all came from a BMW internal factory guide, updated for 1989–96 and 8 Series figures came courtesy of Frank Sutton, BMW (GB) Ltd. American sales stats are prominent in our appendices and were supplied via Andrew Cutler, Corporate Communications, BMW of North America Inc.

Finally I would like to acknowledge the editorial assistance of my wife, Marilyn. She enlivened both the editorial process (particularly original transcript from 1984 for 1997–8) and my life, latterly whilst holding down a stressful job.

Selected Automotive Books Available From Robert Bentley

Enthusiast Books

Unbeatable BMW: Eighty Years of Engineering and Motorsport Success
Jeremy Walton
ISBN 0-8376-0206-8

Volkswagen Beetle: Portrait of a Legend
Edwin Baaske ISBN 0-8376-0162-2

Small Wonder: The Amazing Story of the Volkswagen Beetle *Walter Henry Nelson*
ISBN 0-8376-0147-9

Glory Days: When Horsepower and Passion Ruled Detroit
Jim Wangers ISBN 0-8376-0208-4

Think To Win: The New Approach to Fast Driving *Don Alexander with foreword by Mark Martin* ISBN 0-8376-0070-7

Maximum Boost: Designing, Testing, and Installing Turbocharger Systems *Corky Bell*
ISBN 0-8376-0160-6

Sports Car and Competition Driving
Paul Frère with foreword by Phil Hill
ISBN 0-8376-0202-5

The Racing Driver *Denis Jenkinson*
ISBN 0-8376-0201-7

The Technique of Motor Racing
Piero Taruffi with foreword by Juan Manuel Fangio ISBN 0-8376-0228-9

Race Car Aerodynamics *Joseph Katz*
ISBN 0-8376-0142-8

The Scientific Design of Exhaust and Intake Systems *Philip H. Smith and John C. Morrison*
ISBN 0-8376-0309-9

The Design and Tuning of Competition Engines *Philip H. Smith, 6th edition revised by David N. Wenner* ISBN 0-8376-0140-1

The Sports Car: Its Design and Performance
Colin Campbell ISBN 0-8376-0158-4

Volkswagen Sport Tuning for Street and Competition
Per Schroeder ISBN 0-8376-0161-4

Volkswagen Inspection/Maintenance (I/M) Emission Test Handbook: 1980-1997
Volkswagen of America ISBN 0-8376-0394-3

Harley-Davidson Evolution V-Twin Owner's Bible™ *Moses Ludel*
ISBN 0-8376-0146-0

Jeep Owner's Bible™ *Moses Ludel*
ISBN 0-8376-0154-1

Ford F-Series Pickup Owner's Bible™
Moses Ludel ISBN 0-8376-0152-5

Chevrolet & GMC Light Truck Owner's Bible™ *Moses Ludel*
ISBN 0-8376-0157-6

Toyota Truck & Land Cruiser Owner's Bible™ *Moses Ludel*
ISBN 0-8376-0159-2

Alfa Romeo Owner's Bible™
Pat Braden with foreword by Don Black
ISBN 0-8376-0707-9

The BMW Enthusiast's Companion
BMW Car Club of America
ISBN 0-8376-0321-8

BMW Service Manuals

BMW Z3 Roadster Service Manual: 1996–1998, 4-cylinder and 6-cylinder engines
Bentley Publishers ISBN 0-8376-0325-0

BMW 5-Series Service Manual: 1989–1995 525i, 530i, 535i, 540i, including Touring
Bentley Publishers ISBN 0-8376-0319-6

BMW 5-Series Service Manual: 1982–1988 528e, 533i, 535i, 535is *Robert Bentley*
ISBN 0-8376-0318-8

BMW 3-Series Service Manual: 1984–1990 318i, 325, 325e(es), 325i(is), and 325i Convertible *Robert Bentley*
ISBN 0-8376-0325-0

Audi Official Service Manuals

Audi 100, A6 Official Factory Repair Manual: 1992–1997, including S4, S6, quattro and Wagon models *Audi of America.*
ISBN 0-8376-0374-9

Audi 80, 90, Coupe Quattro Official Factory Repair Manual: 1988–1992 including 80 Quattro, 90 Quattro and 20-valve models *Audi of America*
ISBN 0-8376-0367-6

Audi 100, 200 Official Factory Repair Manual: 1988–1991 *Audi of America*
ISBN 0-8376-0372-2

Audi 5000S, 5000CS Official Factory Repair Manual: 1984–1988 Gasoline, Turbo, and Turbo Diesel, including Wagon and Quattro
Audi of America ISBN 0-8376-0370-6

Audi 5000, 5000S Official Factory Repair Manual: 1977–1983 Gasoline and Turbo Gasoline, Diesel and Turbo Diesel
Audi of America ISBN 0-8376-0352-8

Fuel Injection

Ford Fuel Injection and Electronic Engine Control: 1988–1993 *Charles O. Probst, SAE*
ISBN 0-8376-0301-3

Ford Fuel Injection and Electronic Engine Control: 1980–1987 *Charles O. Probst, SAE*
ISBN 0-8376-0302-1

Bosch Fuel Injection and Engine Management *Charles O. Probst, SAE*
ISBN 0-8376-0300-5

Volkswagen Official Service Manuals

Eurovan Official Factory Repair Manual: 1992–1999 *Volkswagen of America*
ISBN 0-8376-0335-8

Passat Official Factory Repair Manual: 1995–1997 *Volkswagen of America*
ISBN 0-8376-0380-3

Jetta, Golf, GTI, Cabrio Service Manual: 1993–1997, including Jetta///** and Golf**/// *Robert Bentley* ISBN 0-8376-0365-X

GTI, Golf, and Jetta Service Manual: 1985–1992 Gasoline, Diesel, and Turbo Diesel, including 16V *Robert Bentley*
ISBN 0-8376-0342-0

Corrado Official Factory Repair Manual: 1990–1994 *Volkswagen United States*
ISBN 0-8376-0387-0

Passat Official Factory Repair Manual: 1990–1993, including Wagon
Volkswagen United States ISBN 0-8376-0378-1

Dasher Service Manual: 1974–1981 including Diesel *Robert Bentley*
ISBN 0-8376-0083-9

Super Beetle, Beetle and Karmann Ghia Official Service Manual Type 1: 1970–1979
Volkswagen United States
ISBN 0-8376-0096-0

Station Wagon/Bus Official Service Manual Type 2: 1968–1979 *Volkswagen United States*
ISBN 0-8376-0094-4

Fastback and Squareback Official Service Manual Type 3: 1968–1973
Volkswagen United States
ISBN 0-8376-0057-X

Beetle and Karmann Ghia Official Service Manual Type 1: 1966–1969 *Volkswagen United States* ISBN 0-8376-0416-8

Cabriolet and Scirocco Service Manual: 1985–1993, including 16V *Robert Bentley*
ISBN 0-8376-0362-5

Volkswagen Fox Service Manual: 1987–1993, including GL, GL Sport and Wagon
Robert Bentley ISBN 0-8376-0340-4

Vanagon Official Factory Repair Manual: 1980–1991 including Diesel Engine, Syncro, and Camper *Volkswagen United States*
ISBN 0-8376-0336-6

Rabbit, Scirocco, Jetta Service Manual: 1980–1984 Gasoline Models, including Pickup Truck, Convertible, and GTI
Robert Bentley ISBN 0-8376-0183-5

Rabbit, Jetta Service Manual: 1977–1984 Diesel Models, including Pickup Truck and Turbo Diesel *Robert Bentley*
ISBN 0-8376-0184-3

Saab Official Service Manuals

Saab 900 16 Valve Official Service Manual: 1985–1993 *Robert Bentley* ISBN 0-8376-0312-9

Saab 900 8 Valve Official Service Manual: 1981–1988 *Robert Bentley* ISBN 0-8376-0310-2

Robert Bentley has published service manuals and automobile books since 1950. Please write Robert Bentley, Inc., Publishers, at 1734 Massachusetts Avenue, Cambridge, MA 02138, visit our web site at http://www.rb.com, or call 1-800-423-4595 for a free copy of our complete catalog, including titles and service manuals for **Jaguar**, **Triumph**, **Austin-Healey**, **MG**, and other cars.